ITALY

ITALY

BY LEILA MERRELL FOSTER

LUCENT BOOKS
P.O. BOX 289011
SAN DIEGO, CA 92198-9011

Library of Congress Cataloging-in-Publication Data

Foster, Leila Merrell.
    Italy / by Leila Merrell Foster.
        p.   cm. — (Modern nations of the world)
    Includes bibliographical references and index.
    Summary: Examines the land, people, and history of Italy and
discusses its state of affairs and place in the world today.
    ISBN 1-56006-481-1 (lib. bdg. : alk. paper)
    1. Italy—History—Juvenile literature.   [1. Italy]   I. Title.   II. Series.
DG467.F67   1999
945—dc21
                                                                                      98-36878
                                                                                      CIP
                                                                                      AC

Copyright © 1999 by Lucent Books, Inc.
P.O. Box 289011, San Diego, CA 92198-9011
Printed in the U.S.A.

CONTENTS

INTRODUCTION

ALL ROADS LEAD TO ROME—OR, AT LEAST, TO ITALY

Italy is a land of rich historical and cultural significance, the birthplace of Roman law and Renaissance art. It also has given the world much pleasure in the way of popular culture: pizza and Ferraris, designer clothes and internationally acclaimed movies, all have been contributions of Italy to the world. And with its support for the European Union, Italy assures for itself an important place in the twenty-first century.

Over the centuries, the sheer beauty of Italy has attracted artists, poets, and other travelers. The mountains of the Italian Alps, the volcanoes of Etna and Vesuvius, the lake country, the beaches, the lagoons of Venice, and the Blue Grotto

Italy's magnificent scenery, such as this view of the Alps, is just one of the many attractions that draw visitors from around the world.

of Capri, together with Italy's Mediterranean climate, draw visitors like a magnet.

People with varied interests seek out Italy. Sports enthusiasts cite the soccer, bicycle racing, automobile racing, skiing, boating, and swimming that Italy offers. Lovers of fine food want to sample the dishes that vary with the town or city. Scientists marvel at the recent discovery of the five-thousand-year-old body of the Ice Man. Historians explore Etruscan tombs, Roman buildings, museums filled with Renaissance art, and the battlefields of the many wars fought on Italian soil.

Some have personal reasons for coming to Italy. The descendants of Italians who immigrated to other countries during the nineteenth and twentieth centuries want to return to the villages of their ancestors. Soldiers who fought in the hills of Italy during World War II come back to the old battlefields.

Religious reasons attract others to this country. Roman Catholics go on pilgrimage to Rome and to the churches and shrines in other cities. Protestants also have an interest in the art of the early church and in Italian saints, like Benedict and Francis, who contributed to the development of Christian religion. Ancient synagogues and a new mosque attract Jewish and Islamic worshipers.

Many are the reasons for interest in Italy. The saying that all roads lead to Rome can be expanded to include the whole nation.

1

THE BOOT AND WHAT'S IN IT

Italy juts out from the European continent into the Mediterranean Sea, shaped like a high-heeled boot with the toe pointed to the island of Sicily. Other important islands to the west of the mainland are Sardinia, Corsica (owned by France), and Elba. Italy's neighbors to the north are France, Switzerland, Austria, and Germany. To the east, across the Adriatic Sea, lie Croatia, Bosnia and Herzegovina, Albania, and Greece. To the south, across the Mediterranean, are the northern African countries of Tunisia, Algeria, and Libya.

Italy's geographic location helps to explain the importance of the country. In early times, when great civilizations such as Egypt and Greece rimmed the Mediterranean, it was inevitable that the sailors and traders of the ancient world would bump into the boot that was to become Italy.

The mountainous nature of the land encouraged people to form independent, self-reliant units of government. When resources were needed that were not within the natural boundaries of the hills, the people had to go outside in trade or war to secure a supply.

MOUNTAINS AND VOLCANOES

Mountain ranges that are higher than 2,300 feet (702 meters) account for 35 percent of the territory of Italy. The two main mountain systems are the Alps to the north and the Apennines, which run the length of the country like a spine, piercing the island of Sicily as well. A third system accounts for the two large islands (Italian Sardinia and French Corsica) popping up to the west of the mainland.

The Alps have peaks reaching more than 12,800 feet in height, and there are deep valleys formed by glaciers. More than a thousand glaciers are still left, though they are melting. Not nearly as high as the Alps, the Apennines have extinct volcanoes with crater lakes and some active volcanoes such as Vesuvius and Etna.

Vesuvius is the only active volcano on the European mainland. It has a base of about 30 miles (48 kilometers) in circumference with two summits, the highest being 4,190 feet (1,277 meters). Thanks to the eruption of Vesuvius of August 27, A.D. 79, which buried Pompeii and Herculaneum under mud and ash, archaeologists and tourists may visit these historic sites, preserved as they were in the days of the Roman Empire. Two thousand people were killed in the disaster. Other major eruptions have occurred in 1066, 1631, and 1906, and smaller ones in 1913, 1926, 1929, and 1944.

Etna, on the eastern coast of the island of Sicily, is the highest active volcano in Europe. The base covers an area 620 square miles (1,605 square kilometers). Its height, which changes over time, was 10,902 feet (3,323 meters) in the 1990s. The first recorded eruption was in the eighteenth century B.C., and there have been some ninety since, with the last in 1998.

The cone of Vesuvius, the only active volcano on the European mainland, towers 4,190 feet above the city of Naples. In A.D. 79, a massive eruption buried the neighboring cities of Pompeii and Herculaneum under tons of mud and volcanic ash.

Although earthquakes are rare in the Alps and in the Po River valley of northern Italy, the foothills of the Alps experience some strong seismic activity. Severe earthquakes have occurred in the Apennines and on Sicily. In 1997 earthquakes around Assisi, in central Italy, killed eleven and injured over a hundred people. In addition, they damaged irreplaceable art in the Basilica (church) of St. Francis. An earthquake in Naples, to the south, killed twenty-five hundred people in 1980.

PLAINS AND COASTAL AREAS

Plains from river valleys or filled-in sea gulfs account for less than a quarter of the area of the country. The most important plains region lies in the valley of the river Po, which is the country's most fertile growing region.

The seacoasts range from the lagoons of Venice to sandy beaches to high cliffs. One of the most famous winding roads along the high cliffs is on the Amalfi coast. The nearby island of Capri is noted for the Blue Grotto, which is a cave at the waterline. Because most of the sunlight reaching the grotto comes through the part of the cave entrance that is under water, the interior is bathed in an iridescent blue as sunlight penetrates the water. Caves along the coast are a frequent feature and have been used by humans from the earliest times.

RIVERS AND LAKES

While Italy has many rivers, they tend to be short. At four hundred miles, the Po is the longest: from Turin to its outlet on the Adriatic Sea south of Venice, the river can be navigated by boat. The Arno flows through Florence and Pisa. The Tiber is Rome's river.

The rivers in the south can flood during winter storms, yet be bone dry in summer. In 1998 floods overflowing the rivers in the south caused mud slides to bury more than seventy people in a forty-mile area between Naples and Salerno. In the northern and central regions of the country, the rivers tend to be dry during the winter when the headwaters are frozen, but they fill with melting snow in the spring and with rain in autumn.

Italy boasts around fifteen hundred lakes. Most of these are in the Alpine region in depressions formed by glaciers. The most famous are Garda, Maggiore, Como, Iseo, and Lugano. With their semi-Mediterranean climate, these lakes have attracted visitors seeking to avoid the heat of southern Italy and the cold of northern Europe.

BLUE GROTTO

Mark Twain's 1869 description of the famous cave on the island of Capri appears in *The Innocents Abroad:* "The entrance to the cave is four feet high and four feet wide, and is in the face of a lofty perpendicular cliff—the sea-wall. You can enter in small boats—and a tight squeeze it is, too. You cannot go in at all when the tide is up. Once within, you find yourself in an arched cavern about one hundred and sixty feet long, one hundred and twenty wide, and about seventy high. How deep it is no man knows. It goes down to the bottom of the ocean. The waters of this placid subterranean lake are the brightest, loveliest blue that can be imagined. They are as transparent as plate glass, and their coloring would shame the richest sky that ever bent over Italy. No tint could be more ravishing, no luster more superb. Throw a stone into the water, and the myriad of tiny bubbles that are created flash out a brilliant glare like blue theatrical fires. Dip an oar, and its blade turns to splendid frosted silver, tinted with blue. Let a man jump in, and instantly he is cased in an armor more gorgeous than ever a kingly Crusader wore."

CLIMATE, PLANTS, AND ANIMALS

Italy lies in the temperate zone, but because of its great length, there is great variation in climate between the Alpine section to the north and Sicily in the south. Indeed Italy has been divided into seven main climate zones. Average temperature ranges from 43.9°F (6.6°C) with rainfall of 41.5 inches in parts of the north to 64.7°F (18.2°C) with rainfall of 23.5 inches in the southern tip.

Italy is home to almost fifteen hundred lakes. While Garda, Maggiore, and others may be more famous, smaller ones such as Lake Pistono (pictured) are just as beautiful.

The climate provides different zones of vegetation. On the higher slopes, pine and fir trees grow. The lower slopes make room for chestnut, cypress, and oak. The southern and central parts of the country are famous for their olive trees, as well as orange and lemon groves, palm trees, and citrons. Farthest south are fig, date, pomegranate, and almond trees, as well as sugarcane and cotton.

Because Italy has had such a long period of human occupation, there are fewer varieties of animals than are found in other parts of Europe. Marmot, chamois, ibex, wolf, and wild boar still live in the mountainous regions. Bears, which were common in ancient times, are now practically extinct. Foxes frequent the countryside. Birds like the eagle, hawk, falcon, and vulture live in the mountains. Quail and partridge and migratory birds inhabit many parts of Italy. Bats, lizards, snakes, vipers, and scorpions are also present.

Charles Dickens, the famous English novelist who lived for a time around Genoa, described the Italian wildlife thus in 1842:

The view, as I have said, is charming; but in the day you must keep the lattice-blinds close shut, or the sun would drive you mad; and when the sun goes down you must shut up all the windows, or the mosquitoes would tempt you to commit suicide. So at this time of year, you don't see much of the prospect within doors. As for the flies, you don't mind them. Nor the fleas, whose size is prodigious, and whose name is Legion, and who populate the coachhouse to that extent that I daily expect to see the carriage going off bodily, drawn by myriads of industrious fleas in harness. The rats are kept away quite comfortably, by scores of lean cats, who roam about the garden for that purpose. The lizards, of course, nobody cares for; they play in the sun, and don't bite. The little scorpions are merely curious. The beetles are rather late, and have not appeared yet. The frogs are company.[1]

Freshwater fish include the brown trout, sturgeon, and eel. Common saltwater fish are the red mullet and the dentex. In the south, white shark, bluefin tuna, and swordfish can be found, along with red coral and commercial sponge. Local demand for fish is so great that despite increased production, fish are imported from other areas of the Mediterranean, the Black Sea, and the Atlantic Ocean.

RESOURCES

Because the Italian peninsula (the part of the boot surrounded by water) is a young formation in geological terms, it has few minerals. Those that are found are of poor quality and so widely scattered as to be difficult to extract and market profitably. The lack of good supplies of iron ore and coal needed for steel helps to explain why Italy lagged behind some of its European neighbors in developing as an industrial country. Almost all the production of mineral products decreased during the 1980s with the exception of rock salt, petroleum, and natural gas.

With the increasing demand for fuel and energy, the country imports more energy than it exports. Because of the uneven rainfall, it is hard to make electric power from the natural water supply. Most of the sources of water power in the Alps have already been developed. Nuclear power and natural gas have been used to meet energy demands.

Italy's fine white marble is probably the most famous exported mineral resource, though it makes only a small contribution to the country's economy. The quarries in Carrara and Massa in northern Italy produce the best marble, a very hard stone that can be worked only by master artisans. Carrara marble was favored by such famous sculptors as Michelangelo because of its translucent whiteness.

AGRICULTURE

Given the mountainous and hilly terrain of Italy, terracing, irrigation, and soil conservation have been important elements in farming. The most fertile area is the Po valley in the north, where good rainfall helps in the growth of wheat, rice, and corn. Four types of agriculture are practiced: field crops, tree crops, pasture, and forestry.

The hard wheat for making pasta is grown in the south, while the soft wheat for bread and pizza comes more from the northern lowland. Italy exports two other major field crops: tomatoes and rice.

Tree crops from olives and grapes—olive oil and wine—are the biggest moneymakers of the agricultural exports. Most of the citrus crops come from Sicily, while other fruits are the specialties of other regions. Almonds are also a cash crop.

Dairy production is a major industry in Italy's agriculture. Dairy farming (involving cows, sheep, goats, and water buffalo) in the north supports the production of some fifty different kinds of cheese such as Gorgonzola and Parmesan. Products made from goat's milk are considered luxury items, and fine cheeses are an important Italian export.

On the other hand, cattle production is not strong and is threatened by the imports from other European countries. Parma ham is a famous specialty that is exported. Hides are used in the leather industry.

FORESTRY

To make room for crops, housing, and other needs, many of Italy's trees have been cut down. When great numbers of trees were used to construct homes for an expanding population, the root systems were lost, permitting the soil to erode. Increased agriculture made for more soil erosion. Then in the nineteenth century, wood was harvested for use in the mining and railroad industries, further diminishing the country's forest areas.

Most of Italy's remaining forests contain broad-leaved trees such as the beeches, which are fairly well distributed across the country. Conifers account for a fifth of the forest area and are localized in the Alpine foothills. Some areas such as the North Italian Plain, Publia, and the southern part of Sicily have almost no woods.

INDUSTRY

Despite meager iron and coal resources, steel was at the heart of the twentieth-century industrial boom in Italy. After World War II, with liberalization of trade in Europe, steel sparked the growth of industries such as automobiles and precision machinery. Italian appliances, textiles, and chemicals also are prized for their high quality.

The service industry is the major employer in Italy. Over half the working population is employed in tourism, restaurants, transportation, communication, domestic jobs, finance, and public administration. Immigrants from Africa and Asia often fill the positions with the lowest wage and least satisfactory working conditions.

PEOPLE

Most of today's Italian citizens are native-born and have a close association with the region of Italy where they live. The great majority speak Italian, although other languages are used in a few pockets. While 80 percent of all Italians state that they are Roman Catholics, religious minorities (mostly Protestant, Muslim, and Jewish) are guaranteed freedom of worship. Most people in Italy live in towns or cities.

Field-workers sheave wheat in the summer sun. This crop is grown in both southern Italy and in the northern lowlands.

ITALIAN AUTOMOBILES ARE FAMOUS

The Italians entered the automobile industry with the famous Steffanini-Martina in 1896. German, British, and French manufacturers had already begun building cars. Production of Isotta-Fraschini autos began around 1898; these costly, fast, and luxurious cars were classics of the 1920s. Giovanni Agnelli founded Fiat in 1899 and introduced the idea of a small car.

The most expensive standard car was produced by an Italian, Ettore Bugatti, in France in the 1920s. Only six of the Type 41 Bugatti, also known as La Royale, were built.

Automobile racing began in Italy with the Grand Prix run in 1908. Lancia, Alfa Romeo, Maserati, and Ferrari are Italian cars that set the standards in the Grand Prix and Gran Turismo auto races.

After World War II, Italian designs and manufacturers were in demand. Pininfarina of Turin was the best known of the companies. Automobile production in Italy boomed from the 1950s to the mid-1970s, with another increase in the 1980s. More recently, competition from Japan and European countries has been a factor in slowing down sales. However, new markets have opened in eastern Europe.

For many people today, the Ferrari is the dream car. The factory makes only 3,500 cars per year. The new 550 Maranello model goes from zero to 60 miles per hour in 4.3 seconds. It costs $204,000. "This Is *Not* Your Father's Automobile," *Smithsonian* magazine writer Bruce Watson quotes Enzo Ferrari, the founder of the company: "A Ferrari should be longed for and dreamed for. You should have to wait for one like you wait for a star."

Sometimes the country is thought of as having two sections divided by the so-called Ancona Wall, an imaginary line that runs from the port of Ancona on the Adriatic Sea to the southern part of Rome. To the north are the more prosperous larger cities and about two-thirds of the population. To the south is the more rural country, which has fewer people and a more limited economy.

From 1876 to 1970, more than twenty-five million Italians immigrated to other countries, bringing with them their culture and putting their talents to work in other nations. The United States and Canada have large populations with ethnic ties to Italy.

In the past, the boot and the islands that are Italy contained the resources to launch empires. Now Italy must find its way in competition in the European Community and the world at large. Perhaps Italy's greatest resource is the Italians themselves, and their creativity.

From Early Humans to the End of the Roman Empire

In its land and in its climate, modern Italy is very different from the prehistoric region. When water was trapped in glaciers of the Ice Age, land that is now under the Mediterranean Sea may have been exposed. The coastline may have been 12 to 19 miles (20 to 30 kilometers) farther out. Once a narrow stretch of land joined Sicily to the mainland. Evidence that at times tropical creatures roamed the plains and forests of Italy suggests a different climate in those periods. On the other hand, during the Ice Age, the temperature may have been about 48°F (9°C) colder in both winter and summer. Snow may have covered most of Italy for many months.

Early Humans

Italy is rich in the remains of early humans. Around 200,000 B.C., the first human Italians came on the scene. They were probably of the *Homo erectus* type. By 60,000 B.C. the Neanderthals arrived on the scene. The Cro-Magnons may have made an appearance by 10,000 B.C. By 5000 B.C., the climate, plants, and animals were close to their present state in Italy. Agriculture did not take hold until sometime between 3500 to 2500 B.C.

On September 18, 1991, two people hiking along a melting glacier in the Italian Alps stumbled across a body. It was a great surprise to the scientists when the Ice Man, or Otzi as he was nicknamed, turned out to be around five thousand years old. Before this discovery, the oldest glacier victim dated to only four hundred years ago. Scientists studied everything they could about Otzi—his body, his clothing, his possessions. What they learned revolutionized what the scientific community thought about people of prehistoric times.

Italy went through the stages of discovering and using different metals—copper, bronze, and iron. People lived in

17

THE FIVE-THOUSAND-YEAR-OLD ICE MAN

When the body that was to become known as the Ice Man was discovered in 1991, it was cut free from the surrounding glacier with pneumatic drills because no one thought it was anything special. Once scientists at the Institute for Forensic Medicine at the University of Innsbruck in Austria had determined that the body was really five thousand years old, however, the specimen was handled with meticulous care.

Scientists determined that they were examining a short man in his twenties or thirties. He had worn animal skin clothes, a grass cape, and leather shoes stuffed with grass. There were markings on his body that may have been tattoos. The Ice Man had been found at a height of 10,550 feet, which is the highest prehistoric human site ever identified. Not even the remains of campfires have been found any higher.

The Ice Man's copper ax has been of special interest to archaeologists. It is the oldest ax found in Europe with bindings and handle intact. Investigators were especially surprised to discover a copper item in the possession of the Ice Man, since the technology necessary to make it was not thought to exist in the area in 3000 B.C. Every item associated with the Ice Man has been studied. The charcoal that he carried has been analyzed by botanists in an attempt to learn where he might have come from. The fungus the scientists found on a leather thong might have been protection against illness, since it has some antibiotic properties. Who was this person? His clothing and tools show that he was a mountaineer. Perhaps he was a shepherd, a trader, or even a religious shaman, who needed to go into the mountains. He appears to have frozen to death.

When the significance of the discovery was realized, Italy claimed the Ice Man. Surveyors proved that he had been discovered 303 feet inside Italian borders. However, the Austrian police had salvaged the remains, and Austrian scientists had worked to preserve the materials. An agreement was finally reached that Ice Man would be left in Austria until studies had been completed. In 1998 he was returned to Italy in a refrigerated truck to be shown in a refrigerated case in a special museum in Bolzano, a city in northern Italy.

villages—sometimes in houses built on piles or stakes over water. Different groups built impressive tombs and burial monuments, many of which remain today to impress tourists. From earliest times waves of people came into Italy as traders or settlers. Among the most famous traders were the Phoenicians, based on the eastern shore of the Mediterranean. These skilled builders and sailors of boats had a big colony in Carthage on the African coast. The Greeks also looked on Italy as a good base for trade for their exports of bronzes and pottery, but they made settlements as well.

Greek settlers introduced the systematic cultivation of grapes and olives. They also contributed an improved alphabet that made writing easier. They are responsible for naming Italy from the word, *Fitalia*, meaning "land of cattle," which was appropriate for the southwest coast of Italy in the fifth century B.C. Although the Greek culture was far in advance of that of Italy of this period, the Greek cities were so busy fighting each other that they failed to take advantage of the opportunities Italy presented.

THE ETRUSCANS

The most important people before the Roman Empire were the Etruscans, who lived along the northern west coast, which is now known as Tuscany. Scholars have long debated whether the Etruscans sprang from the population then inhabiting the territory or whether they migrated from elsewhere in around 700 B.C. In any event, not long after their appearance, they organized work crews to clear the land for crops and cities and to build roads.

Where geography permitted, Etruscan city streets were laid out on a grid plan. Wealthy people in these cities had two-story homes built around a courtyard. Even the family tombs were often laid out in rows, like streets. The tombs of the leaders were sometimes shaped like houses and the walls were often painted with murals. Good pottery, metal objects, and jewelry also were buried with the dead.

The Etruscans placed carefully determined sacred boundaries around their cities, and indeed, religion was a major factor in their life. These early Italians believed in many gods and spirits, although three of major importance correspond to the later Roman deities named Jupiter, Juno, and Minerva

An Etruscan stronghold rises above the ancient city of Veii. A highly organized society, the Etruscans built their cities along gridlike patterns, with streets and even tombs arranged in straight rows.

(the king and queen of the gods and the goddess of wisdom). Religious rituals specified how people were to act in public and private, how to build temples, how to organize cities, and how to fight wars. They made human sacrifices to their gods. Sometimes the victims were forced to fight each other to the death as gladiators. Livy, a Roman historian, called them "a people who above all others were distinguished by their devotion to religious practices."[2]

ETRUSCAN CULTURE AND SOCIETY

Religion was one of the main factors that bound the various Etruscan cities together. Leaders of twelve cities met at times for joint actions, but the cities maintained a high degree of independence. They had a common art and culture. In addition to the tomb and pottery painting, they turned out fine metalwork. Music and dancing were much appreciated. The Etruscans were great traders and sailors. Etruscan coins were minted from the end of the sixth century B.C.

The classes of the society were strictly segregated. The Etruscan warriors who took control of an area did not mix with the local people. The aristocracy enjoyed both wealth and status, living in great luxury, while the common people had little. The kings had crowns and thrones and used as a symbol of power a collection of fasces (rods) that was to become a Roman symbol and still later was adopted by the Fascists of twentieth-century Italy.

Unlike women in many ancient cultures, Etruscan women had high status and freedom. Women owned property and kept their own names rather than taking those of their husbands, practices that allowed children to inherit goods from the maternal side of the family. Women entertained with their husbands and were often buried with them. They were depicted in art together with their mates. This prominence of Etruscan women scandalized the Greeks and Romans. A modern scholar, Professor Larissa Bonfante, thinks that the status of these northern women was very threatening to Greek and Roman males, not only accounting for their dislike of Etruscans but constituting "Rome's first 'cultural shock.'"[3]

FALL OF THE ETRUSCANS

One way of managing tensions in this highly structured society was the constant expansion of the Etruscans to new ter-

Exploring Etruscan Tombs

In the 1950s Carlos Lerici wanted to study Etruscan underground tombs because some of them have paintings on the walls, sculpture on the sarcophagi (limestone coffins), and burial objects that will tell a great deal about the life of these little-known ancient people. However, there were thousands of tombs. How could he find and explore the most interesting sites without wasting a great deal of time?

Lerici studied aerial photographs, looking for any differences in the landscape that might indicate man-made structures underground. Then he tested below the surface by passing energy (sound, pressure, radio waves, or electric impulses) through the soil to detect any tomb or cave that might be below. Finally, to avoid digging up thousands of tombs, he bored a 3-inch (8 centimeters) hole and put down a tube with a periscope head and a light. When he needed to take pictures, he attached a camera to this device.

As a result, Lerici was able to examine scientifically thirty-five hundred tombs. Although most were empty, twenty had painted walls. Lerici left many tombs almost undisturbed to allow later archaeologists to investigate how the structures were built, or to explore any other questions that may arise in connection with some new theory. Most important, however, is the knowledge about burial customs and how Etruscan society was organized that has resulted from a scientific study of the tombs.

ritory along the western coast. By the early part of the sixth century, the Etruscans had occupied Rome, pushing as far south as Campania. Three Etruscan kings ruled in Rome from 616 to 510, turning it into a real city with advancements in culture, drainage, and buildings.

Not all Etruscan contributions were positive, however. The last of the kings has been portrayed as a cruel tyrant, and his son is infamous for having sexually assaulted the wife of a leader in whose home he was a guest. The incident, known in art and literature as "the rape of Lucretia," triggered a rebellion that contributed to the Etruscans' downfall.

Aristodemus, the leader of the Greek settlement of Cumae, blocked Etruscan expansion into southern Italy by preventing the Etruscans taking the city, which was about twelve miles from what is now Naples. The Etruscan fleet was lost in a battle off Cumae in 524, signaling the end of Etruscan power in the south. In the north, a short period of Etruscan domination on the other side of the Apennines and into the Po valley was brought to a halt with an invasion in 400 B.C. of Celtic tribes coming down into Italy. The Romans, enlarging their territory from the south, took control of the last Etruscan city in 265 B.C.

The Etruscans had come very close to bringing about a unification of the Italian peninsula. They had brought great

According to legend, the founders of Rome were Romulus and Remus. They were raised by a female wolf, and the scene of them being nursed by the animal (pictured) has come to be one of the symbols of Rome.

progress to the territory by founding cities, spreading their alphabet and culture, and developing structures of religion, politics, and warfare. However, they failed to create a single nation because their independent cities often refused to act together and because of consistent rebellions against the Etruscans' harsh treatment. Their structured society concentrated a disproportionate amount of power and wealth in the hands of a few. As the Etruscans extended their domain, the few public officials who were empowered to act decisively were not enough to ensure control over the territory already held. Their final defeat was to come at the hands of the Romans.

MYTHS OF THE RISE OF ROME

Rome was the first great empire in Italy. As Rome achieved power over most of the world that Romans knew, her people developed stories that would account for the greatness of their civilization.

Romulus and Remus were said to be two children of Rhea Silvia, the daughter of a king named Numitor, and Mars, the Roman god of war. To escape a wicked uncle, the boys were put on a raft in the Tiber River. They ended up in the area now known as Rome, where according to legend they were adopted by a female wolf. This scene of the children being nursed by the wolf has become one of the symbols of Rome. Instructed in human ways by a shepherd, the boys later set out to found a city—Romulus choosing the Palatine hill, and

Remus, the Aventine hill—two of the seven hills for which Rome is famous. Romulus killed Remus and so started Rome on the Palatine hill.

Another story was that Aeneas, prince of the city of Troy on the eastern coast of the Mediterranean, escaped when the city fell to the Greeks. After a dangerous journey that is described by the Roman author Virgil in the *Aeneid*, the hero made his way to Italy, where he married a princess called Lavinia. This story can hardly be true, since the Trojan War took place some four hundred years before Rome was founded, but it was accepted by the early Romans. Like Romulus and Remus, Aeneas was believed to be the son of a human and a mythologic deity.

Some early Roman historians put the two traditions together so that Romulus becomes the grandson of Aeneas. In this version, Romulus founded Rome on April 21, 753 B.C., and then had to find women to inhabit his new city. He invited a local tribe, the Sabines, to a celebration and stole their women, an event imaginatively depicted by many a later artist. Romulus reconciled with the Sabines and ruled for a while with the king of the tribe, Titus Tatius.

ROMAN GOVERNMENT

While these ancient legends cannot be validated, it is likely that a person named Romulus was the first in a line of kings. Romulus was succeeded by Numa Pompilius, a Sabine, who established a period of stability, divided the land among Rome's citizens, and established religious ceremonies and a twelve-month calendar. The kings had overall power of Rome, but they could not pass the title to their sons. Rather, the ruler was selected according to religious standards, and experts, called diviners, checked on omens, or signs, that the gods might send. The social organization was based on extended families, with the father having unlimited power over everyone else in the family.

Romulus, the first king of Rome. While not the same person as that found in myth, he assumed the throne during the eighth century B.C.

When the last Etruscan king was overthrown, the Roman Republic was established about the year 509 B.C. Now the power that the king had was shared by two men, called consuls, elected by the people for a single term of one year. The consuls were chosen from the Senate and returned to that body when they had finished their consulship. To counter

Gaius Octavius, later known as Augustus, took control of Rome in 44 B.C. He also held control over the army, an authority which gave him the powers of an emperor.

the power of the Senate and the aristocrats (called patricians), the less privileged classes, called plebs, organized themselves and elected tribunes to protect them. The power of the plebs lay in mass protests and threats of refusal to support the government; later, laws were passed that permitted them to hold power.

As Rome struggled to rule an ever-expanding territory, an ambitious war hero named Julius Caesar assumed dictatorial powers. Although offered the kingship by one of his followers, he knew that it was good politics to turn it down. When he was murdered in 44 B.C. by other leaders who had conspired against him, a power struggle broke out. The winner, Gaius Octavius, who was the great-nephew of Caesar, was given the title of Augustus and was also known by this name. In 31 B.C. Augustus took over the task of restoring order. In theory, he as chief (called *princeps*) shared power with the Senate. Because he controlled, financed, and ordered the army, however, Augustus had the power of an emperor and was able to name his successor. This new system allowed Rome to govern its empire, but often at the cost of freedom for individual citizens.

ROME'S EXPANSION

From the city that Romulus supposedly established to the great empire that stretched from Britain to Egypt, Rome's expansion depended on the government of its territories and the effectiveness of its armed forces. Instead of keeping the Etruscan system of isolating its conquered peoples, Rome attempted to incorporate them by giving them at least partial rights as citizens or by treating them as allies. Often the Romans supported the ruling classes against local uprisings, increasing the leaders' dependence on Rome. Roman citizens who did not own property were given land in the conquered territories and encouraged to settle there. By the end of the period of the republic, Rome had conquered the Italian peninsula and unified it, although it was not until 27 B.C. that the emperor Augustus officially incorporated the territory north of the river Po into the empire.

Rome's greatest rival during this early period was the city of Carthage in North Africa. Between 264 and 146 B.C. there were three wars against this enemy, the so-called Punic Wars. During the first war, the Romans kicked the Carthaginians out of Sicily. From fifty thousand to seventy thousand men were involved in the armies and navies of these two powers. It was during the second war that the Carthaginian general Hannibal attacked the Romans in the rear, coming over a pass in the Alps with elephants. In 202 B.C., the Romans attacked and pinned down Hannibal, while Scipio, one of their greatest generals, defeated the Carthaginians. This war was the beginning of the expansion of Rome into the region around the Mediterranean. However, Carthage still remained a threat, so in 147 B.C. Rome sent another general named Scipio to North Africa to finish the job. He captured the city, killed the inhabitants, burned what remained for ten days, and then scattered the earth with salt so that it would not be productive.

Whether in North Africa or in Europe, Rome's Wars were not easily won. The tribes to the north were a threat and massacred as many as eighty thousand men in 105 B.C., terrifying the Romans. Revolts broke out in conquered territories such as Spain. Pirates attacked Roman shipping. A general named Pompey, who achieved fame by clearing the sea around Rome

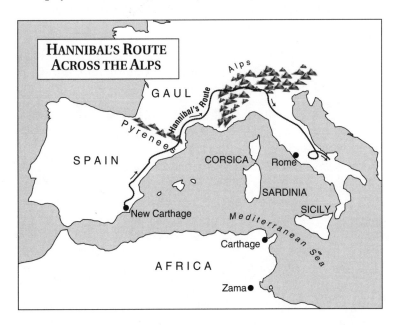

of the pirates, went on to add the territory around the Turkish and Syrian coast to Rome. Yet after these significant contributions to the empire, Pompey saw his forces defeated by Julius Caesar, who had won great victories in Gaul (modern France) and would later conquer other territory.

During the period of empire between 70 A.D. and 235, Rome's boundaries were at their broadest, stretching from Britain in the northwest to Arabia in the southeast. Allied kingdoms such as Egypt and Judea were taken over as possessions. The armed forces kept the peace. The system of roads and water transportation permitted the transport of goods and also ideas. Rome was the capital of this great empire.

ROMAN CULTURE

Building on Etruscan foundations and borrowing from their neighbors, the Greeks, Romans set about living the good life. The wealthy ordered spacious homes for themselves. The forum—the center of civic celebrations in Rome—was enlarged and beautified. Arches, columns, and other monuments to victories were erected. Public baths and theaters were built. Temples, including the Pantheon, a huge, domed building, were dedicated to the gods the people worshiped. Great sports arenas, such as the Colosseum, provided the public with a place to watch gladiators kill each other and wild animals. This building boom went on throughout the empire.

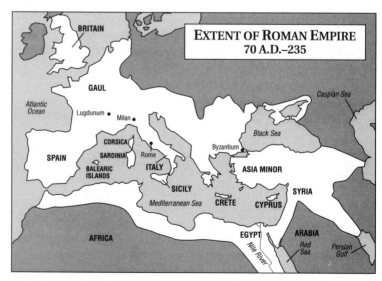

Very little of Roman painting survived the centuries. Although the Romans followed and copied the Greek sculpture, they are known for especially good portrayals of heads. Roman mosaics (pictures made of small pieces of stone or glass) are found throughout the empire.

Writers flourished. Tacitus wrote history. Virgil told the story of Rome's founding in the *Aeneid*. Juvenal specialized in satire. Cicero's speeches were collected. Poets such as Catullus and Lucretius were honored. Many Romans had grown wealthy as a result of trading and shipping opportunities offered by the powerful empire. Thus they had the funds to support these homegrown writers, artists, and architects, and the leisure to appreciate their work.

ROMAN RELIGIONS

From as early as the seventh century B.C., Romans honored a sky or water god who had importance to farmers; and his wife, who was in charge of the life of women. Certain Etruscan and many Greek gods and goddesses also were worshiped. Eventually, some of the Roman emperors were hailed as gods and had their own cults. Piety, for the Romans, was not so much an individual spiritual experience as the observance of rituals designed to benefit the entire community by winning the favor of the deities, who would then grant prosperity, harvests, and success in war.

Empire brought the Romans in contact with Middle Eastern gods. Some of the foreign religions promised more personal benefits. Secret initiation ceremonies and rites were often an important element of such cults. Isis was an Egyptian goddess with a large following in the Greek world. Mithra, a Persian god for men only, was very popular in the army. Jews were found throughout the empire, and their beliefs were generally tolerated and even admired for their moral and ethical basis.

Christianity was a special problem for the Romans. At first, they considered it a form of Judaism. But when Christians refused to sacrifice to the pagan gods, and talked of Jesus as a king, they were singled out for persecution and death. However, the Christian community continued to grow. The message of the worth of every human—slave or free, Jew or Greek, male or female—attracted many in an empire made up of distinct classes and rival ethnic groups. Another factor

Though of humble birth, Diocletian rose to the position of emperor and instituted many reforms. He also split Rome's territories into two parts in an attempt to preserve the empire.

that brought in outsiders was the care extended by Christians to all members of their community.

ROME'S DECLINE

With so much in its favor, how could Rome decline? In 235 the emperor Severus and his mother were murdered by Roman troops. The next fifty years were marked by power struggles as some twenty-one emperors were on and then off the throne. At the same time, barbarian tribes threatened the empire in the north, in the east, and across the Mediterranean in Africa. One of the tribes from the north reached Milan in northern Italy before being turned back. Then the emperor, Valerian, decided to try to halt the decline by dividing the empire into two parts, with the hope that the smaller units could be managed more easily. This action hastened the decline of Rome.

There was no strong Roman ruler after the death of Valerian for over twenty years. But in A.D. 284, soldiers put on the throne a man of humble origins who had a very high opinion of himself—Diocletian. During his twenty-year reign, Diocletian reformed the economy, the army, and the political system. He split the empire into two parts, east and west, and then again in two, by giving power in the Balkans to one person and in Gaul and Britain to another. While these reforms preserved the empire for a little longer, it was necessary to increase taxes to pay the additional government workers required to make the system operate, with problems for the economy as a result.

When Diocletian retired in 305, the empire was in for another period of uncertainty until Constantine took over as emperor in 324. Constantine maintained the division of the empire into eastern and western parts until his death in 337, giving control of each part to one of his sons. Constantine is known for the founding of Constantinople as his eastern capital in what is now Turkey. He also was the first head of state to convert to Christianity. In 312 Constantine interpreted a vision of a cross against the sun as a sign that if he embraced Christianity, he would win a crucial battle. He indeed prevailed at the Milvian Bridge near Rome, and Christianity was officially recognized as a religion in 313. Persecution of Christians stopped except for a brief pagan revival under another emperor, and Christianity became the dominant religion of the empire. While strong emperors like Diocletian and Constantine were able to give some stable periods of government, the decline resumed with weak leadership.

THE FALL OF THE ROMAN EMPIRE

The eastern section of the empire, with its capital at Constantinople, survived as the Byzantine Empire, although it became more Greek than Roman in emphasis. The western, or European, section continued to fall apart. The emperor moved his court north to Milan in 305 and on to Ravenna, another northern city, in 402. The barbarian tribes in various parts of the

In this carving, Constantine is shown after his conversion to Christianity (note the figure holding a cross above his head). He founded the city of Constantinople, which became the capital of the eastern Roman Empire.

empire were conquering territory that had once belonged to Rome. Then in 410, Alaric, the leader of a Germanic tribe called the Visigoths, captured and sacked Rome itself.

The barbarians wanted territory and riches. Rome was a good target. Ammianus, a soldier and a historian, reported that the nomads that came from the steppes of Central Asia were no good at fighting on foot "but are perfectly at home on their tough, ugly horses. . . . It is on horseback that each one of this people buys and sells, eats and drinks, and bent across the narrow neck of his steed, takes a deep sleep." He called them the "most fearful of all warriors." [4]

The Visigoths sack Rome after its capture in 410 A.D.

Many scholars have come up with reasons for the fall of Rome. According to the editors of Time-Life Books, "more than 200 factors have been cited as contributory causes. They have ranged from the predictable—including political intrigue, economic mismanagement, religious division, corruption, top-heavy bureaucracy, immorality, and civil wars—to the surprising, such as climactic change and the recently discredited theory of widespread mental erosion caused by poisoning from lead water pipes and eating utensils." [5] The overexpansion of the empire and the overdependence on conquered people, together with poor management, would go far in explaining Rome's problems.

The lengthy period from the settlement of the land 200,000 years ago by early humans to the fall of the capital of the powerful Roman Empire in 410 saw much progress, as well as a series of rising and falling cultures. Basic lessons of civilization learned during these times were passed along to the next generations of people to inhabit Italy.

From the Breakup of the Empire to Reunification

For fourteen centuries, Italy was in fragments, though at times some of the parts were very powerful and influential. City-states blossomed into empires. The Renaissance—a time of rebirth of culture—began in Italy and spread to other parts of Europe. On the other hand, Italy was subject to foreign domination and had to fight to become a unified country, recognized in the modern world.

For some eight hundred years, the city of Rome had been free of attacks by foreign invaders. But on August 24, 410, when Alaric and his army of Visigoths entered Rome and looted the city, the significance of this defeat was felt across the Roman Empire. Rome itself was not of great importance from a political or military standpoint. No emperor had lived there since 312. Rather, the success of Alaric encouraged other northern tribes to finish off the dying empire. The last Roman emperor in the west was pushed from his throne by Odoacer, a barbarian general commanding Germanic troops supposedly in the service of Rome. Another barbarian fighter, Theodoric, killed Odoacer in 493. Theodoric built a palace at Ravenna and gave Italy a period of peace until his death in 526.

FOREIGN ATTACKS TO THE END OF THE MIDDLE AGES

Throughout the period after the fall of Rome until the unification, Italy was subject to attacks from foreign nations and powers. At first, the Byzantine (eastern) emperor began an invasion of the country to reunite Rome with Constantinople. Then the Lombards from northwest Germany crossed the Alps in 568, took over most of the Po valley, and pushed on into the central and some of the southern part of the country.

This balance was upset when the popes, fearing the power of the Lombards, called for help from the Franks, in what is

Lombard warriors invade the city of Pavia in 572 A.D. In an attempt to stop the marauders, the Roman popes enlisted the help of Frankish king Pepin and his son, Charlemagne.

now France. The Frankish king Pepin and later his son, Charlemagne, defeated the Lombards and took over some of their territory. Then, in 827, Sicily was attacked by Arabs seeking additional territory under the influence of their new Muslim faith. In 846 Arabs sailed up the Tiber River and sacked some outlying churches, scattering the bones of saints and martyrs. The greatest extension of Arab power in Italy was around 900. The Franks and Arabs were later replaced by the Germans and the Normans.

The new superpower in Europe was a German king named Otto I, who invaded Italy in 951 and 961 and controlled much of the northern and central parts. Meanwhile, the Normans, tough military fighters descended from the Vikings but speaking French, were brought in to fight in some of the wars of the independent groups in the south. Discovering that there was more profit in seizing territory for themselves, the Normans fought the Byzantines and the Arabs and, with the capture of Palermo in 1072, brought all the territory of southern Italy into the western Christian sphere. The language of this area now switched to a form derived from Latin rather than Greek or Arabic. The population came to accept the Roman Catholic Church rather than Islam or the Greek Orthodox religion.

TRADING CITIES

The fragmentation of Italy gave cities a good deal of independence—an important factor in the development of international trade. The cities situated on the Mediterranean had ports that gave them access to trade with Europe, Africa, and Asia. Venice, Bari, Amalfi, Salerno, Naples, Gaeta, Pisa, and Genoa took advantage of this opportunity. Some of these cities acquired significant foreign territories, which they controlled and used to reprovision their ships.

Merchants in these cities acquired wealth. They and the skilled workers of the city formed guilds, banding together for strength and protection. These people of the emerging middle class challenged the old upper class for political power and formed organizations for sharing wealth, responsibilities, and plans for great buildings.

The trading operations of the Italian cities help to explain why a Marco Polo would leave Venice to find a route to China and back and why a Christopher Columbus of Genoa would want to find a sea route to China. Such explorers were looking for new markets in which to buy and sell goods.

A wealthy merchant tours the waterfront which brought him his riches. Port cities such as Venice, Genoa, and Naples were vital links to trade routes connecting cities in Europe, Africa, and Asia.

Charlemagne, who helped defeat the Lombards, was rewarded by Pope Leo III with the crown of the Holy Roman Empire.

PAPAL POWER

After the defeat of the Roman Empire, the cities had to develop their own defenses. Because the Senate had not survived as an effective political unit, the people of the city of Rome looked for help to their bishop, the pope. As early as Gregory the Great (590–604), the popes had been exercising political power by feeding people, making peace treaties, and paying troops. The independence of Rome suited the popes well because it enabled them to avoid having to follow orders and directions of the Byzantine emperor. Also, it gave the popes a larger role in Europe, where they sent missionaries to bring Christianity to the barbarian people.

However, it was often the popes, fearing that they would be swallowed up by foreign invasions, who called on other foreigners for help. To reward kings who came to their aid, the popes often bestowed additional titles on their rescuers. Thus, for example, on Christmas Day 800, Pope Leo III crowned Charlemagne, who was already king of the Franks, as Holy Roman Emperor. However, the idea of one European ruler, legitimized by the pope, caused many other ambitious men to come to Rome, attempting to secure the crown for themselves. They often destroyed Italy's crops and wealth in the process.

When the pope awarded the crown to Otto I, the German king, in 962, the end result was a loss of papal power. During the next few centuries, Germany took a keen interest in the politics that usually surrounded the office of the popes, sometimes intervening at the highest level of papal affairs.

Otto III (983–1002), who lived in Rome for much of his reign, allowed the pope little political power.

In the second half of the eleventh century, a strong reform movement swept the church. Questions were asked about the use of government or family power to influence decisions relating to priests or other religious matters. The popes began to assert their control. The matter came to a head in a feud between two strong rulers, Pope Gregory VII (1073–1085) and Emperor Henry IV (1056–1106). In 1077 the pope excommunicated the emperor and made him beg for three days in the cold courtyard of a castle of Canossa in northern Italy before receiving him again as a church member. Henry responded by having his German bishops elect another pope, invading Rome in 1081, forcing Gregory into exile, and having the new pope crown Henry emperor. This squabble ended in a compromise with the emperor's forces still appointing church officials but church providing the ritual that symbolized the office.

The twelfth century saw the Normans consolidate their gains into a strong state, only to be ousted by a German family, the Hohenstaufens. The middle section, the Papal States, was held by the popes, who frequently had to play the north off against the south. In the north, the German emperors attacked the wealthy city-states, which enjoyed a great deal of independence and fought each other when not under attack by the Germans. This balance of power was a factor in the uncertain days that followed.

The period between the fall of Rome in about A.D. 500 and the start of the Renaissance in about 1500, is often called the Dark Ages—a time when the light of learning went out and

Popes Gregory the Great (lower left) and Gregory VII (lower right) were two church figures who exercised their political influence by helping the poor, keeping the peace, and paying the troops of Rome. Sometimes these activities caused conflict between the popes and their emperors.

had to be rekindled. However, many scholars disagree with this name, citing numerous cultural achievements.

For example, the great sixth-century churches of Ravenna were built during the reign of Gothic tribes from the east. A reforming priest named Benedict created the religious order that bears his name to govern his monastery at Monte Cassino. The monks helped to preserve books and learning. Benedict's sister, Scholastica, started a convent. Gregory the Great, as pope, instituted reforms of the church and guidelines for pastoral care. Great churches in the Romanesque style were built, decorated with frescoes and mosaics. The medical school at Salerno achieved fame. Judges and lawyers in Bologna made that city important. Poetry in the common language rather than old Latin or Greek became popular. Religious orders were founded by men and women who were later raised to sainthood: Francis, Clare, and Dominic. The Franciscans and the Dominicans sent preachers to the common people. The theologian Thomas Aquinas became a great teacher of the church. Benedict, Thomas, and Scholastica are now revered as saints.

SHIFTS IN THE THIRTEENTH CENTURY

The death of Emperor Frederick II in 1250 began a period of shifting power. Frederick's heir, Manfred, held the position of king of Sicily. Pope Urban IV, a Frenchman, encouraged his countryman Charles of Anjou to contest Manfred for at least part of the empire. Charles killed Manfred in 1266 and took control of Sicily. He then defeated and beheaded Frederick's grandson, ending the Hohenstaufen reign. In 1282, however, France lost Sicily to Spain.

On the Italian mainland, two parties formed that split the loyalties of the nobles. The Guelfs supported the pope against the emperor. The Ghibellines supported the emperor. Cities took sides depending on how their interests would be best served.

Thanks to his political maneuvering, Pope Boniface VIII (1294–1303) managed to offend the people of Florence, the Franciscan friars, and the Spanish king in Sicily. The king of France, Philip IV, gave support to the enemies of the pope, who arrested Boniface in 1303. Boniface died in that year, but a successor, Clement V, who also was French, moved the papacy from Rome to Avignon, in southeastern France. For nearly seventy years, Avignon, not Rome, was the base of operations of the popes.

GOVERNMENT IN THE CITIES

It is estimated that by the fourteenth century, twenty-three cities had populations exceeding twenty thousand and roughly four hundred claimed some form of autonomy. The cities, however, depended on the rural areas for food, labor, and supplies. In each city opposing groups, or factions, fought among themselves, but also made alliances with other factions in their own and other cities.

During the fourteenth century, many of the popular and democratic institutions that had been effective in the cities were changed in favor of a more centralized government. Sometimes control was held by one man who was the head of one of the major families. Sometimes a group of powerful men, the signori, exercised power.

There were several reasons for this shift from democratic forms of governing. For example, less authoritarian regimes had been weak and unable to respond to fighting among the factions. Moreover, the economy was bad, forcing bankruptcies. Food was in short supply. And the Black Death, an epidemic of plague that hit the cities of Europe hard in the mid–fourteenth century, caused millions of fatalities.

When these calamities struck, strong leaders took control and often were able to bring stability to uncertain and frightening situations. While some of the democratic legislative bodies were kept by the signori, they were effectively controlled. Since the leaders acted in their own interest, the wealth became concentrated in the hands of the ruling family, who then had funds to spend on increasing their prestige through new buildings and new works of art.

By the end of the fourteenth century, the five principal powers in Italy, each with a population between 800,000 and 2 million, were the republic of Venice, the republic of Florence, the duchy of Milan, the Papal States, and the kingdom of Naples. Since further expansion by any of the five would have been very difficult, the group created the Italian League in 1455. While there were some smaller independent states, they were allied with one of the major five powers. The nearly forty-year period of peace that followed provided an important stimulus for the growth of art and literature.

THE BLACK DEATH

The plague that first hit Europe between 1347 and 1351 came from China and inner Asia. Some Asiatic troops fighting a trading post of Genoa located in the Crimea catapulted corpses, victims of the illness, into the town. As a result of this low-tech version of germ warfare, the plague spread rapidly to Mediterranean ports and on into Central Europe. The illness recurred in 1361–1363, 1369–1371, 1374–1375, 1390, and 1400.

The disease, which is carried by fleas that have bitten infected rats, caused more deaths than any other epidemic or war up to that time. More people died in towns and heavily populated areas than in the countryside. Between one-eighth and two-thirds of the population of different areas died. It is estimated that in Europe twenty-five million people died and some thousand villages were wiped out. The population of western Europe did not regain its pre-1348 level until the beginning of the sixteenth century.

In Italy the death toll was so severe that some towns and fields were abandoned. Those who survived generally had more wealth. Labor was needed to rebuild. This demand gave the lower classes a power that they had not enjoyed before. Because of the shortage of labor, landowners were forced to give wages or rent to keep people on the land in place of requiring labor from them. Wages increased for craftspeople and peasants. The result was to bring some flexibility to a society that had been completely lacking in opportunities for advancement by the lower classes.

In this woodcut, a plague victim points to one of the deadly swellings covering his body. His doctors stand by, unable to help.

VENICE, FLORENCE, AND MILAN IN THE RENAISSANCE PERIOD

Venice had an empire in the Mediterranean and the largest navy. The head of this mighty city-state was called the doge. Doge Tomasso Mocenigo reported that in 1423 the fleet was made up of 3,000 small ships with crews totaling 17,000, as well as 300 large sailing ships manned by 8,000. Through trade and a banking system, the city grew steadily. Venetians sailed north to Germany, Scandinavia, and England. To the east, they claimed ports along the Adriatic and into the Aegean Sea. With crusaders arriving from all over Europe en route to the Holy Land, Venice turned a good profit and extended its power on the eastern shores of the Mediterranean. Unfortunately the trading ships also brought home disease, and the city suffered some twenty-two outbreaks of plague.

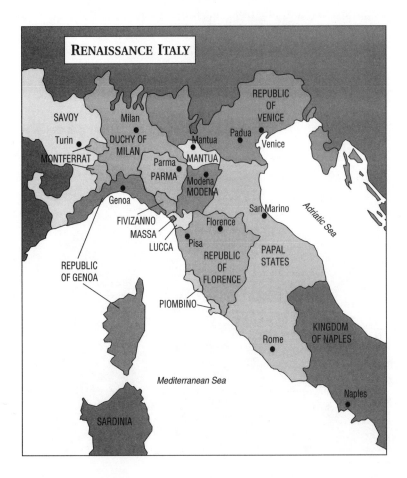

This richest of all the cities reached its peak at the beginning of the sixteenth century. When Portuguese navigators discovered the route around Africa to reach India, Venice lost its control over the rich spice trade and began a slow decline.

The success of Florence was based on the cloth trade—especially wool cloth. The wool guild employed six thousand people. The Florentines also became the leading European bankers and lenders. The city's gold florin, minted in 1252, became a major European currency. A family of bankers, the Medicis, supplied two of the most important leaders: Cosimo the Elder (1389–1464) and Lorenzo the Magnificent (1449–1492). The Medicis supported the arts and the daily pageants and festivals for which the city was famous. A very different kind of leader, Girolamo Savonarola (1452–1498), a Dominican friar, preached against idle amusements and immorality in all forms. At first, the Florentines gave Savonarola great support but later turned against him and had him burned at the stake on the basis of confessions of false prophecy obtained under torture. The Medicis extended their power, and in 1513 Giovanni de' Medici became Pope Leo X. Art and architecture flourished in Florence under Medici rule.

The city of Florence as it appeared during the height of the Renaissance. Florence became the center of commerce during the sixteenth century.

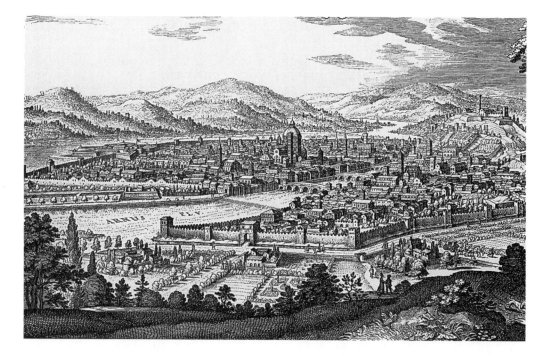

In Milan the Visconti family held absolute power. Gian Galeazzo (1351–1402) was the most notorious member of this family, killing off relatives who challenged him and marrying a succession of female relatives to extend his power through their alliances. He was on his way to conquer all of Italy when he died of fever. However, he was a good administrator. His economic policies and construction projects stimulated industry. Dairy farming and crop farming grew with improved irrigation. The silk industry employed some fifteen thousand people. The Visconti dynasty came to an end, and the Sforzas, another important Milanese family, fell from power for lack of an heir, whereupon the French took over the city.

THE PAPAL STATES IN THE RENAISSANCE

The Papal States went through a long period of decline. From 1309 to 1378, the popes were in exile in Avignon, France. Without strong central control, the various cities that made up the Papal States went their own way. One of these city-states, San Marino, on the Adriatic side of the peninsula, remains independent of Italy to this day. The city of Rome was in decay, though still fought over by local families. Catherine of Siena, the patron saint of Italy, played a role in convincing Pope Gregory XI to return from Avignon to Rome. When the papal court came back to Rome, there was another crisis. Pope Urban VI angered the cardinals who had elected him, so they elected another pope, who chose Avignon as his base. Eleven years later, a third pope was elected and established himself in Pisa. The matter was finally sorted out in 1417, when Martin V was elected pope and returned to Rome.

Martin V began the work of rebuilding Rome and restoring control over the Papal States. His successors followed his policies. One of the greatest popes of this period was Julius II, who had ambitions for a great reign in Rome and wanted to control all of Italy. His new buildings changed Rome more than any innovations at any time since the Roman emperor Augustus. Rome, with a population of some hundred thousand, became a major city, attracting scholars and artists.

THE KINGDOM OF NAPLES IN THE RENAISSANCE

The old kingdom of Sicily was now divided between the Spanish, who controlled the island and the French, who

The ruins of the colosseum in Rome. During the fourteenth and early fifteenth centuries the city had fallen into a state of physical and political decay, a situation that was reversed by the election of Martin V as pope in 1417.

controlled the mainland. The mainland section was to become known as the kingdom of Naples. Its ruler, Robert of Anjou, was called Robert the Wise and was honored throughout Italy. Under his governance, Naples and its university became a world-famous center of culture.

However, the kingdom was sparsely populated and dependent on agriculture for its wealth. The peasants were oppressed and lived in great poverty. The economic problems of the fourteenth century hurt agricultural prices, and the population declined drastically. After Robert's death in 1343, the nobles fought and even became bandits raiding the countryside. Sicily faced a similar situation after the death of its ruler in 1377.

Then, asserting a Spanish claim to the territory, Alfonso of Aragon in Spain took leadership and was able to unite the island and the mainland. Naples regained some of its reputation for being a center of learning. After Alfonso's death, his son responded with such cruelty to an invasion by a Frenchman, revolts by peasants, and a mutiny by his nobles that Italian nobles in exile encouraged Charles VII of France to invade the kingdom and take it over. Charles did so, but then went back to France. The territory then came under control of the Spanish.

Renaissance means rebirth, and while this period of history did not have much influence on the economy of Italy or change the lives of most Italians, it had a huge effect on the upper classes. The heritage of ancient Rome and Greece was rediscovered and given new life; both the intellectual and the artistic cultures were changed.

On the intellectual side, new schools were developed to promote the training of the privileged men in society. With wealth concentrated in the hands of a few, the sons of the leaders could take time to study history and ethics and develop skill in rhetoric—speaking effectively. Scientists turned to observing nature. Libraries were founded to encourage learning. Perhaps the best representative of the "Renaissance man"—a well-rounded person—was Leonardo da Vinci (1452–1519), who was a great painter, a scientist, and an inventor.

In art, a new style emphasizing the realistic depiction of human forms became popular. While most of the artists were craftsmen from the middle class, the orders for their work came from wealthy individuals and institutions.

REFORMATION AND COUNTER-REFORMATION

The new learning of the Renaissance also affected the church. Protestant reformers such as Martin Luther and John Calvin tried to reform or correct church teachings that they believed were dangerously misguided. For example, Luther preached against the sale of indulgences, documents that relieved purchasers of certain punishments for their sins. Money from these sales funded church projects such as the rebuilding of St. Peter's Basilica in Rome.

Some of those who criticized or protested abuses in the church became known as Protestants. The Protestants separated from the papacy to form their own churches. The Roman Catholic Church responded forcefully in an effort to protect its teachings and the power of the pope to define them. Under this Counter-Reformation movement, the reformers were met with harsh treatment by the Roman Catholic Church in Italy and in other countries.

The popes tried to achieve uniformity of thought by publishing an Index of Prohibited Books that banned the possession, reading, sale, or transmission of many works. Among these were important political and literary writings by Italians such as statesman Niccolò Machiavelli and the poet Dante. The ideas of Italian scientists were challenged. Galileo Galilei, the world-famous astronomer, mathematician, inventor, and philosopher, was tried and imprisoned in 1633 for contradicting the church's view that the earth was the center of the universe. Galileo's belief, later shown to be correct, was that the earth and planets revolve around the sun. Other scholars were burned at the stake. Many intellectuals fled Italy for countries in which they could express their ideas in greater freedom.

One side effect of this persecution was the channeling of creative efforts into safer fields. Thus Italy produced an unusual number of brilliant painters, sculptors, architects, and craftsmen. Music was another safe enterprise. Italian com-

RENAISSANCE ART

Great Renaissance art is found in Italy because it was the Italians who had the wealth and the interest to commission artists to create it. The artists developed unique styles and pioneered new techniques.

In the early Renaissance, artists experimented with showing figures in real-life settings, both in the round and in depth. They also perfected an ancient technique called fresco, in which scenes are painted on a thin layer of damp, newly applied plaster. Ideal for large surfaces, frescoes show strong colors to great advantage. Among the giants of the Italian Renaissance of the fourteenth and fifteenth centuries were the painter and architect Giotto di Bondone, and the sculptors Lorenzo Ghiberty and Donatello.

The so-called High Renaissance featured use of realism even in religious subjects. Among the great artists of this fifteenth through sixteenth-century period were Michelangelo, Leonardo da Vinci, and Raphael.

In the mid–sixteenth century, art entered a period called "mannerism" when more contorted and imaginary treatment was given to subjects. The paintings of Venetian artists Titian, Tintoretto, and Veronese are representative of this style.

A close-up view of Michelangelo's Sistine Chapel painting shows the artist's magnificent use of realism to portray his subjects.

posers invented the art form known as opera, the first opera performance occurring in 1600.

Although Michelangelo and other geniuses received public acclaim for their works, many of which were expressions of the artists' religious faith, it is also true that possession of these magnificent creations enhanced the prestige of the wealthy patrons who had paid for them.

Foreign Domination and Decline

The period of peace and independence that had fostered the flowering of learning in the Renaissance came to an end with the sack of Rome in 1527. This destructive rampage by the soldiers of Charles V, the Hapsburg king of Spain, the Netherlands, and Austria, was allowed to run its course because the slowness of communications in those days prevented the ruler from controlling his troops. Charles was also Holy Roman Emperor, and therefore most of Italy was incorporated into his empire, which stretched from Vienna, in Austria, to the Spanish colonies in South America.

Italian territories were given by treaty to the Spanish branch of the ruling Hapsburg family. Most of the remaining Italian states owed their status to Spanish support. Only Venice was free, and the Renaissance lived on there until about 1600. The rest of Italy was milked for whatever Spain needed to achieve her ambitions in the world.

The Spanish Hapsburg line, which died out in 1701, was replaced by rulers from the Bourbons, a noble family of France. Then at the Peace of Utrecht in 1713, Italy was shuffled over to Austrian Hapsburg control while still a part of the Holy Roman Empire. For two and a half centuries, until the French invasion of 1796, the people of Italy were governed by foreign rulers, who also taxed them heavily. Only Venice and the Piedmont region in the northwest avoided these overlords.

The French invasion of Italy, led by Napoleon Bonaparte, caused nearly twenty years of upset, beginning with the partition of the country between France and Austria, which had been at war with each other. In this division, in 1797, Venice was assigned to Austria, thus ending that city-state's centuries of independence. The rest of northern Italy went to France.

In a message on New Year's Day, 1797, General Bonaparte said: "Italy unfortunately has been long excluded from the number of European powers. If the Italians today are worthy of resuming their rights, some day they will see their country appear with glory among the powers of the earth."[6] He then established two Italian republics: the Cisalpine in Northern Italy and the Ligurian around Genoa.

Almost immediately, however, Bonaparte departed for Egypt. During his absence, other parts of Italy declared themselves republics. Their independence was short-lived. A combination of Austrian and Russian armies and Italian peasants combined to quash the new republics and to drive the French occupiers out of most of the peninsula. The setback displeased Bonaparte, who had wanted control over Italy for the sake of the crops and soldiers the country could provide. Thus upon his return from Egypt, he expelled the Austrians from most of the Italian territory they had held. In 1804, he dispensed with the republican form of government and became emperor of France. The next year he had himself crowned king of Italy.

Italy remained under French control until 1815, when Napoleon's European enemies defeated him at Waterloo. The Congress of Vienna, an international body convened to dismantle the empire Napoleon had constructed, apportioned the various Italian states to the major powers. The Austrian leader Prince Klemens von Metternich, referring to Italy as "merely a geographic expression,"[7] put an end, at least temporarily, to the dream of a unified Italy.

RISORGIMENTO—RISING AGAIN

In the period following Napoleon's defeat, some forces worked at reestablishing power and institutions that had been in control before while others started small uprisings that turned out to be ineffective. Intellectual support for Italian political unity came from the English poet Lord Byron, an Italian playwright, Silvio Pellico; and even composers of operas such as Giaocchino Rossini and Giuseppe Verdi. Other leaders wrote books and organized support. The patriot Giuseppe Mazzini established an organization called Young Italy for persons under forty years of age; there were monthly dues, and each member had to have a dagger, a rifle, and fifty cartridges. Vincenzo Gioberti, a liberal priest from Turin who was in exile in Belgium, published a book urging the creation of a state to be governed by a group of princes led by the pope—an approach favored by moderates. Count Camillo

Cavour was the editor of *Il Risorgimento*, a newspaper in the Piedmont region of northern Italy. The paper's name, which means rising again or resurrection, captured the imagination of Italians, as did the editor's call for independence and a league of Italian rulers against the Austrians.

Revolution of 1848 and What Followed

The mid–nineteenth century saw revolutions break out in France and Austria, and the unsettled times seemed to offer a chance for change in Italy. An uprising in Milan and Venice

Napoleon: Liberator or Thief?

When Napoleon invaded Italy, many residents saw him as a liberator. He brought to Italy such ideals as liberty and equality. He built schools, roads, and public projects. He reformed the financial system and the bureaucracy. He introduced a clear code of laws, the Napoleonic Code, based on the belief that all citizens should be equal under the law.

Most important, he brought the idea of a united Italy to people's attention by showing that political boundaries could indeed be swept away. Italians wanting national freedom could look back to what Napoleon had accomplished as a model for future dreams. During the Napoleonic period, a middle class began to develop, which would gain the power to influence political goals.

On the other hand, Napoleon took many famous Italian art works back to Paris. He forced Italians into his armed forces, and used Italy's food resources. He increased taxes. Some scholars feel that he disrupted gradual Italian unification that might have proceeded more smoothly than the Risorgimento.

Napoleon's rule of Italy was both good and bad. He established reforms but looted many works of art and increased taxes.

in 1848 ultimately had almost all of Italy up in arms. The Austrians fought back, however, crushing resistance everywhere except in Venice and Rome. The Italian revolutionaries failed largely because they were not able to act in a unified way and lacked good tactical sense.

In Rome, a new republic had been established that had sent the pope packing to Naples where he urged Roman Catholics to send troops to end the uprising and restore his territory. Troops from both Naples and France responded. Mazzini went to Rome to lead the government there. The job of defending the city was given to Giuseppe Garibaldi, who had acquired experience in guerrilla warfare during a period of exile in South America. At first, Garibaldi prevailed over the French, but his troops were defeated when the French returned in massive force.

Meanwhile the Austrians attacked Venice with bombs dropped from balloons. With food running short in Venice and the deadly diseases cholera and typhus sweeping the city, the Venetian leader, Daniele Martin, had to surrender. Martin went to Paris in exile; Garibaldi, who had retreated to Venice after his defeat in Rome, fled to America. Austria was in control of Italy again.

Milan burns during the revolution of 1848. This uprising failed, however, when the Austrians fought back and crushed the Italian resistance.

GIUSEPPE GARIBALDI, HERO OF THE RISORGIMENTO

While many talked about and plotted for the independence of Italy, Giuseppe Garibaldi led the forces that achieved this victory. Born in the city of Nice, now in France, on July 4, 1807, Garibaldi was a sailor for ten years and in 1832 earned a certificate entitling him to act as a merchant ship captain. He served in the navy of the kingdom of Piedmont–Sardinia. In 1834 he took part in a mutiny that was part of a republican revolution. He escaped to France when the plot failed, but he was condemned to death in his absence.

In exile in South America in 1843, he took command of a group of Italians who were fighting for Uruguay in a war of liberation from an Argentinian dictator. The men of this unit called themselves "Red Shirts," a name that was to be associated with the followers of Garibaldi. In South America, the Italian leader learned the tactics of guerrilla warfare, which he used effectively later against European armies.

Garibaldi led sixty members of his Italian Legion back to Italy to fight in 1848 in the war of independence against the Austrians. He fought in other parts of Italy—Milan and later Rome. Still the Piedmontese would not let him return to his family after the Battle of 1849, so he went into exile again, traveling between Peru, Tangier, in Morocco, and Staten Island, in the United States.

When he was allowed to return to Italy, Garibaldi was given the rank of major general in the Piedmontese army. His greatest achievement was his conquest of Sicily and Naples, which he accomplished without government backing. Garibaldi's request to continue governing the south was refused because he was thought to be too dangerous a rebel. According to *The Horizon Concise History of Italy* by Vincent Cronin, he later told a friend, Admiral Carlo Persano: "This is what happens, Persano, they just treat men like oranges, pressing out the juice to the last drop, and throwing the peel away."

Garibaldi was much admired outside Italy. Abraham Lincoln offered him a command in the Union Army during the Civil War. The offer was rejected because it was not the supreme command and because Garibaldi felt that Lincoln was not going far enough in condemning slavery. This revered Italian patriot died in Italy in 1882.

For the next decade, the leaders of the revolution were to work from the Piedmont, in northern Italy. Cavour cultivated the friendship of the French leader, Napoleon III, and promised France the territory of Nice and Savoy from the Piedmont in return for French help in ousting the Austrians. Victor Emmanuel II, the Piedmont king, wanted a united Italy. Five thousand men from various parts of Italy joined the Piedmontese army, Garibaldi returned from America, and Martin in Paris approved the movement. Their efforts were unsuccessful, however. The battles of 1859 in the north were so bloody that Napoleon III made peace with the Austrians.

ATTACK THROUGH THE SOUTH

Mazzini, in exile in London, recognized that an approach beginning in the south represented a better route to independence. Thus he sent a friend, Francesco Crispi, to Sicily to encourage rebellion there.

Additional fighters were needed for such an enterprise, however, and Garibaldi recruited 1,089 volunteers, who arrived in Sicily on two barely seaworthy vessels. The recruitment itself was a spectacular achievement, for Garibaldi, having failed to obtain support from his recent allies in the Piedmont, raised the thousand-plus troops on the basis of his personal reputation as a brave Italian patriot.

Garibaldi took Sicily with great loss of life, but a steady stream of new volunteers signed on to the cause. He then crossed to Naples and took that city. Cavour in the Piedmont had been concerned that Garibaldi would continue on to liberate Rome and draw the French into fighting. To discourage France from entering the hostilities, Cavour obtained French approval of an arrangement whereby the Piedmont would take over some of the Papal States while leaving Rome to the pope.

Fighting flared up in Naples again and was put down by Garibaldi in October 1860 at the Battle of Volturno. Afterward, when Garibaldi met Victor Emmanuel II, the king of Piedmont, near Volturno, he greeted him with words that have become famous: "I salute the first king of Italy!"[8] And indeed, in 1861 Victor Emmanuel received the crown of a nearly united Italy.

Not everyone was happy with what followed. Mazzini, who had done so much with his young Italy movement, was disappointed with the monarchy. He had hoped that Italy would turn out to be a republic—ruled not by a king but by the people. Garibaldi, who had become very popular and wanted to play a role in Sicily, was now considered a danger to the new kingdom and was denied the governmental post he wanted. Cavour decided that the captured territories would be added to the kingdom of Victor Emmanuel by having the people vote—that is, by a plebiscite. The vote was overwhelmingly in favor of joining, thereby uniting most of Italy by 1861. Venice and environs were still Austrian, and the pope still claimed Rome, but Venice was annexed in 1866. Four years later, the pope's French supporter Napoleon III was deposed, and Italy took the opportunity to seize control of Rome.

The fragmentation of Italy that had lasted for fourteen centuries after the fall of the Roman Empire had been overcome in political union. However, economic differences remained between the wealthy north and the resource-poor south. Of the 26 million inhabitants of the new kingdom, 78 percent were illiterate. Moreover 70 percent of the adult population was engaged in agriculture, putting Italy far behind many European countries in industrial development. A strong Germany on the other side of the Alps was to be a source of worry. The young, united Italy faced many problems in the century ahead.

4

ITALY IN THE TWENTIETH CENTURY

For Italy to have survived in the twentieth century with all its problems is a major achievement. Not long after realizing unification under a monarchy, the country was taken over by a dictator. After a painful period, the dictator was deposed and executed. The present republican form of government has encountered its share of problems. Italy fought on the same side as the United States and Canada in World War I and was their enemy in World War II. Now Italy faces the problem of merging her economy into the fledgling European Union.

FORMING THE NEW KINGDOM

With all the different perspectives in the nation—city and country, liberal and conservative, rich and poor—the task facing the leaders was described by Massimo D'Azeglio, a former prime minister of the Piedmont kingdom: "We have made Italy; now we must make Italians. . . . To make Italy out of Italians, one must not be in a hurry."[9] Roads, railways, schools, and industries had to be developed. People who had almost no experience with democratic government, trade unions, and a free press had to learn how to use these unfamiliar institutions. The mere formation of the nation, important as that might be, did not mean that the inhabitants automatically would work well together.

Cooperation was complicated by the behavior of a nineteenth-century pope. Angry over the loss of his power over Rome in 1870, Pius IX shut himself up in the Vatican (his palace in Rome) and forbade Italian Catholics to take part in Italy's government, either as voters or as officeholders. Moreover, 1870 was the year in which Pius IX issued the doctrine of papal infallibility declaring that popes could not be wrong when they spoke with authority on matters of faith and morals. The response of the Italian government in 1871 was to make the clergy subject to all laws that affected the citizens.

The first legislature of the new government was elected by three hundred thousand voters out of a population of about twenty million; it split into two parties. On the right were moderates from the Piedmont, with support from others, and on the left, people who had supported the ideas of Mazzini and Garibaldi for a republic. At first, the right took power and worked at establishing the rules for the new nation and providing a better economy. In 1876 the left came to power and held a majority for about thirty years, with the result that the two-party system was destroyed and the left split into many factions. The party was held together by arrangements some referred to as bribery, according to which supporters were rewarded with important positions and other advantages.

Sometimes the prime minister handled domestic problems in dictatorial ways. Troops were used to break up riots. Labor associations and a new political party, the Socialists, were outlawed. Dissatisfaction was shown in more riots in 1898, and the assassination of King Humbert in 1900. Although another King, Victor Emmanuel III, was duly installed, the new prime minister, Giovanni Giolitti, took power in the government and held control of the ruling party from 1900 to 1914. He backed legislation that improved labor, public health, and housing. Business prospered. Even agricultural workers saw their lives improve. The many Italians who had emigrated to the Americas from 1870 to 1914 sent money back to their relatives. The arts were flourishing. The operas of such native composers as Verdi and Puccini were produced. Movie companies began production in Rome, Turin, and Milan. Some thought of this period before World War I as a wonderful era.

Giovanni Giolitti assumed power as prime minister in 1900 and held this position for fourteen years. Italy flourished during his time in office, and many improvements were made in labor, public health, housing, and agriculture.

FOREIGN POLICY BEFORE WORLD WAR I

An increasingly powerful Germany lay just beyond the Alps, and enemies had invaded Italy from that direction many times before. It was the fighting between France and Prussia (now a part of Germany), in which Italy sided with Prussia, that won for the Italians the territory of Venice. However, Italy was not happy with developments on the international front. Her claims to Trentino on her northern boundary were rejected. Then the French seized the North African city of Tunis, which Italy wanted to control because many Italians had settled there. In 1882 Italy joined Germany and Austria-Hungary in a pact called the Triple Alliance.

Mazzini's friend Francesco Crispi, who became prime minister of Italy in 1887, decided that to keep up with other European countries, his nation needed colonies in Africa. First he invaded and took over Eritrea and Somaliland (now Somalia) on the Red Sea. Then, in 1890, he declared Ethiopia to be under Italian control. However, this mountainous country was more difficult to subdue. When Crispi ordered an attack in 1896 to complete the conquest, more than ten thousand Italians were killed or captured. The shocked nation forced Crispi to resign.

In 1911–1912, Italy seized the former Turkish colony of Tripoli and renamed it Libya. This military operation hurt the economy at home, however, and as World War I approached, Prime Minister Giolitti advised the country to remain neutral because Italy was not ready to fight.

ITALY IN WORLD WAR I

Italy did remain neutral in 1914 when Germany and Austria declared war against France and Russia and Great Britain declared war on Germany, but the call to empire was still strong. Moreover, Italy wanted to obtain territory, then in Austrian hands, that had been part of the Venetian empire. When it was obvious that Austria would not give up this land, Italian diplomats decided to back France and England, whose spokesmen promised in secret that if victorious, they would give the territory in question to Italy. This secret agreement, known as the Treaty of London, was signed in 1915. Italy's participation in a war against Germany and Austria did not violate any commitments associated with the Triple Alliance because that agreement did not require Italy to support these nations in a war of aggression.

The Italian troops who fought in World War I were inadequately trained, poorly armed, and badly led. However, they attempted to defend the difficult northern boundary, and they attacked Austrian territory in the northeast. When German and Austrian troops could be shifted from the Russian front, they defeated the Italians in that territory and marched on toward the peninsula. The Italians stopped the enemy advance at the river Piave and were reinforced by British and French troops, which helped to push the Austrians back north. Italy regained lost territory and added the South Tyrol in the north of the country, an area formerly held by Austria.

At the Versailles peace talks in 1918, held at the end of the war to decide the fate of the losers and divide the spoils among the winners, the Italians won the South Tyrol and some land with few resources in North Africa. However, the territory promised to Italy in the secret pact was not handed over. United States president Woodrow Wilson would not recognize the secret agreement and felt that for the newly formed country of Yugoslavia to succeed, it had to be awarded the Dalmatian coast on the Adriatic. Angered about the loss of Dalmatia and the control of the Adriatic Sea, Italy permitted the poet and statesman Gabriele d'Annunzio to lead a volunteer occupation force in the city of Fiume (Rieka) on the Adriatic coast, which the Italians held for a year. In a treaty with Yugoslavia, Fiume eventually became an Italian city, but this gain scarcely compared with the dream of all Dalmatia, which although only 28 miles wide had 233 miles of Adriatic coastline.

Italian troops prepare to leave for the Austrian frontier during World War I. Suffering from poor leadership, training, and armament, Italy's forces relied on the help of British and French troops in the defense of their homeland.

POSTWAR TENSIONS

Changing a wartime economy to a peacetime footing can be difficult. In Italy, unemployment and inflation were high, and strikes were common. In this tense atmosphere, strong groups arose on both sides: Communists on the left; Fascists on the right. Communists wanted to abolish private ownership of the means of production, and to give more power to the workers. Fascists wanted both workers and management under government control.

Inspired by the success of Bolshevik (Communist) revolutionaries in Russia in 1917, Italian workers seized control of

Black-shirted members of Benito Mussolini's Fascist party raise their standards during a political rally. Feared for their criminal methods, the Fascists were nevertheless seen by the public as the only means of protecting Italy from communism.

factories in 1920 and tried to run them for their own profit. Giolitti, who was back in power, did not send in troops; he just let the experiment fail. The chaos that resulted made people look to the Fascists to bring some order to the country.

The Fascists, led by Benito Mussolini, at first were in favor of nationalist and socialist policies—support for Italy and government-owned business. Then Mussolini found that backing from business owners was more useful, so his group fought against the Socialists, who wanted government ownership. The Fascists, dressed in black shirts and organized into squadrons, used gangster tactics to break strikes and blow up labor headquarters. However, many people saw them as the only hope of protection against communism.

FASCISTS IN POWER

In 1921 Mussolini and thirty-four other Fascists were elected to the legislature on a platform of sound finance, a strong state, social reform, strike breaking, and rigid control of the economy within a framework of private ownership. The Socialists called a general strike in 1922, and the Fascist Black Shirts broke it up. The Fascists took over government buildings. King Victor Emmanuel asked Mussolini to form a government, which he promptly did. For the next twenty-three years the Fascists were in control, with the king as head of the nation in name only.

At first, people were hopeful, believing that Mussolini would be more moderate than most Fascists. While he did put an end to some of the extreme actions of his followers, he gave Italy a totalitarian government, ending all political opposition and freedom of the press and forcing industry into what he called the "corporate state." No strikes or lockouts were allowed. Owners and workers had to settle disputes in special labor courts. Mussolini, known as il Duce (the Leader), appointed a council of eighty persons to assist him. He had a talent for giving emotional speeches that could move large crowds. His motto became: "Everything within the state. Nothing outside the state. Nothing against the state." [10]

THE LATERAN PACT

Although not a devout Catholic, Mussolini saw the church as a supporter in his battle against chaos and communism. Thus he began talks with Pope Pius XI to attempt to persuade the pontiff to recognize the Italian state, something the popes had withheld since 1870, the year Italy took Rome.

In 1929 Pius XI and Mussolini signed the so-called Lateran Pact, named after the papal palace in which the two leaders finalized the agreement. According to the terms of the pact, the pope, speaking for the church, recognized Italy as a legitimate nation; in return, the Italian government agreed to allow instruction in Roman Catholicism to take place in state schools and to recognize church marriages as legal. In addition, the church received a substantial financial benefit in the form of state bonds. However, the Fascists refused to exempt the clergy from the general ban on criticism of the regime, for they considered the state to be the supreme authority in government. With silence from the clergy and the Fascist recognition of the church, many people gained the impression that the Roman Catholic Church supported the Italian dictatorship. Yet it was not only the church that he wanted to control; Mussolini had visions of a new world empire.

MUSSOLINI'S INTERNATIONAL ACTIVITIES

Mussolini's dreams of world leadership are reflected in a speech he made on October 25, 1932, to an audience in Milan: "I say to you, that the twentieth century will be a century of fascism, the century of Italian power, the century during which Italy will become for the third time the leader of mankind."[11] Also, he saw war as a noble and natural activity.

In 1935, Mussolini declared war on Ethiopia, a country Italy had unsuccessfully attempted to seize in 1890. Ethiopia and Italy were both members of the League of Nations (an international organization that preceded the United Nations). To protest this aggression, fifty-one League member nations voted to impose limited economic sanctions on Italy. Those sanctions did not include two of Italy's most essential needs: oil and coal. This left Mussolini free to bomb Ethiopia and release poison gas on civilians. In May 1936, he announced the fall of Ethiopia to cheering crowds in Rome.

Mussolini also sent almost a hundred thousand troops to Spain in 1936 to fight on the side of dictator Francisco Franco and the Nationalists in the civil war there. He justified the move by claiming to be saving a Roman Catholic country from the threat of communism, which denies the existence of God.

MUSSOLINI AND HITLER

Adolf Hitler, the Nazi dictator of Germany, had encouraged Mussolini's attack on Ethiopia and had also supported the Spanish Nationalists. After Hitler invaded Austria in 1938, Mussolini invited him to Rome. The two leaders entered into the Pact of Steel. The German–Italian alliance created what was called the Axis. Italy had fallen out of favor with Great Britain and France with its Ethiopian campaign, so the new pact showed the world that Italy could make friends with an important power like Germany. The Axis shortly would oppose the Allies, composed of other European countries, England, the United States, and Canada, in World War II.

In many ways, Mussolini followed the lead of Hitler, whom he described as a madman. For example, he passed laws that took away many of the rights of Jews. He had his army march

BENITO AMILCARE ANDREA MUSSOLINI

The man who was known as il Duce was prime minister of Italy from 1922 to 1943 and the first of the world's twentieth-century fascist dictators.

He was born on July 29, 1883, in Predappio, Italy. The oldest child of the local blacksmith, he made political use of his lower class background and identified himself as a man of the people. However, the Mussolinis, while poor, might well be considered to be a middle-class family, since the father was also a journalist and the mother a schoolteacher.

Mussolini as a child was such a bully in the village school that he was sent to a boarding school run by the Salesians, a strict Roman Catholic order. There, he stabbed one of the pupils with a penknife and attacked a teacher. He was expelled and sent to another school, which he also had to leave because he assaulted another pupil with his penknife.

Mussolini was intelligent, however, and he passed his examinations and obtained a teaching diploma. Soon deciding that teaching was not for him, he went to Switzerland, where he read widely, began writing and speaking, and made a name for himself by calling for strikes and violence. He was arrested several times and put in prison. Soon he had the reputation of being one of the most talented, if dangerous, of Italy's younger Socialists. However, he changed his mind about socialism and decided to argue for simply advancing Italy's interests. He became the editor of a newspaper.

During World War I, he was wounded while serving with a corps of sharpshooters. When he was discharged, he gathered men who were to become the nucleus of a political party. He called his group the Fasci di Combattimento, saying that they were to be bound together as tightly as the rods, or fasci, that symbolized ancient Rome. His supporters wore black shirts. His speeches, while often factually incorrect, held audiences with their emotional power.

During a nationwide work stoppage in 1922, Mussolini promised that if the government would not stop the strike, the Fascists would. The Fascists marched on Rome, and the king called on their leader to be prime minister. At thirty-nine years of age Mussolini became Italy's youngest prime minister.

During the years before World War II, Mussolini managed to achieve a peace and unity for his country that permitted economic growth and social reforms. He might have been considered a hero if he had not plunged Italy into disastrous wars, beginning with his battles for colonies and ending with his alignment with Hitler in World War II. His death by execution on April 28, 1945, was mourned by few Italians.

Mussolini and Adolf Hitler together in June 1940. Italy's "Pact of Steel" with Nazi Germany was made in the hope that it would bring Rome worldwide recognition and gains in territory.

and salute in the Nazi manner. And in 1939 he attacked Albania—a country across the Adriatic from Italy that had little to offer except additional territory.

At first, Italy remained a "non belligerent," or nonfighting, nation; that is, the Italian state supported Hitler in ways other than militarily. But as Mussolini watched Hitler's gains during 1940 in Denmark, Norway, the Netherlands, and Belgium, he decided to get into the war as Germany's ally in order to gain some territory. When the Nazis approached Paris in 1940, Mussolini declared war on France as an ally of Hitler. He thought that Hitler would win a quick victory, and he wanted to be eligible for territory at any surrender of the Allies. As he explained his action to one of his generals: "All we need is a few thousand dead" to gain a place at the peace conference.[12]

ITALY IN WORLD WAR II

The Nazis never fully trusted Mussolini and did not tell him in advance of their decisions to take Romania and to attack the Soviet Union (Russia and other Soviet states). Believing that two could play at that game, Mussolini attacked Greece without consulting Hitler. The war went badly for the Italians, and the Nazis had to come to their rescue more than once. Italy sent a force of 110,000 to fight on the Russian front in 1942, but lost half the men—some were killed in battle, many perished in the bitter cold. The Italian navy was not equipped to fight a twentieth-century war. Lack of air cover weakened it further.

The military defeats were accompanied at home by food shortages and Allied bombing. Public opinion turned against the Fascists. Opposition was expressed in strikes in the Turin factories, supported by Anti-Fascist groups such as the Communists. When the Allies landed in Sicily in 1943, Mussolini was forced to give up his powers by the vote of the Fascist Grand Council. Mussolini chose to ignore the vote, but he

An American soldier stands in the ruins of a bombed-out church in Italy in 1943. The fight for Italy was a difficult one, with Allied forces battling the Nazis for control of the peninsula after the Fascist government surrendered.

was arrested by the king and imprisoned. Soon afterward Victor Emmanuel III signed an armistice (an agreement to stop fighting) with the Allies.

Germany, however, could not allow Italy to fall to the Allies. Thus in 1943 the Nazis invaded Italy and took all except the southern part, which was held by the Allies. They rescued Mussolini and had him set up a new government in the north. Average Italian men and women had to decide whether to join their fellow citizens who were resisting the Germans or to fight in the Fascist Black Shirt brigades. At its peak, the Italian Resistance consisted of two hundred thousand people. (When the war ended in 1945, however, a far greater number of Italians would claim to have been part of the Resistance.)

Like other armies in history, the Allies discovered that the fight for Italy was not easy. The May 1944 battle for Monte Cassino was particularly hard fought, for the Germans had converted the Benedictine monastery into a fortress, which they defended to the death. But Rome was liberated in June, and guerrillas took over Milan, Turin, and Genoa. While the Resistance forces suffered heavy losses from the Germans, they probably saved these northern towns from further damage by the retreating Nazis. Mussolini tried to flee to Switzerland but was captured at Lake Como. The Italian Communists in the Resistance ordered him shot, and his body was hung upside down in Milan.

With victory, the Allies faced the problem of securing the peace. In a 1947 settlement, Italy lost her colonies in Africa and some less important territory. In addition, Italy was ordered to make payments to England and the United States to compensate for wartime losses. The former Allies did not accept the money, however. Indeed, America supplied a great deal of aid to Italy after the war, to help the country cope with the devastation.

POSTWAR POLITICS

The postwar problems were many. The armies and the bombing had wrecked Italy: homes and factories, schools and churches, hospitals and universities, roads, bridges, and railway lines had been destroyed or badly damaged. Priceless historical and cultural assets were lost, as well. Resources were scarce, and prices shot up. Unemployment was high, for there were few jobs outside the agricultural sector.

THE ALLIED FIGHT FOR ITALY 1943–1944

SWITZERLAND
AUSTRIA
HUNGARY
ITALY
YUGOSLAVIA
Pisa
CORSICA
Allies enter Rome
June 4th, 1944
1944
Adriatic
Sea
Rome
Anzio
Cassino
ALBANIA
1943
SARDINIA
Naples
1943
Salerno
1943
Mediterranean
Sea
Messina
1943
SICILY
1943
TUNISIA
Allied Drives

The country was still divided over ideas. In the north and central part, where many leaders of the Resistance had been communists or socialists, the foundation was built for a strong Italian Communist Party backed by trade unions and other workers' groups. The south was more conservative and more influenced by the Roman Catholic Church. There support existed for a political group that tried to build on some of Mussolini's ideas.

Thus Italy developed strong postwar factions on both the left and the right. There were centrists, as well: people who feared that right-wing extremism would lead to dictatorship and that the left would force the country into communism with links to the Soviet Union. The Christian Democrats and a number of small liberal groups constituted the center. Its leader, Alcide de Gasperi, was the first Roman Catholic prime minister of Italy since the unification. He held office for five years—a time of stability that allowed the country to recover and rebuild its economy.

THE REPUBLIC

What form of government would Italy choose after the war? An election took place on June 2, 1946, when members of a consti-

THE BATTLE FOR ITALY IN WORLD WAR II

Foreign correspondents covering the war reported on the devastation they saw in Italy. One such report was filed by journalist Homer Bigart, to the *New York Herald Tribune* on May 20, 1944, and appears in *Italy in Mind*, edited by Alice Leccese Powers. "With the 8th Army in Cassino, Italy, May 19—Cassino is a bleak, gray, smoking ruin, which, with a little sulphur added, would be more grim than a Calvinist conception of hell.

The city, when we entered it at 12:30 P.M., was silent. For the first time since January no shells crumped down amid the skeleton walls of the few score buildings still erect.

I have seen all the devastated towns on the road to Rome—Capua, Mignano, San Pietro, San Vittore and Cervaro. But not even ghostly San Pietro compares with the utter ruin of this key citadel of the Gustav [German defense] line.

This once prosperous district center of 15,000, roughly midway between Naples and Rome, is a phantom place of windowless shops and crumbled hotels. Not one Italian crawled from the ruins to cheer the British troops pressing onward for the battle against the Adolf Hitler line. Even in San Pietro part of the population remained, but here in Cassino none could have endured the four hellish months of siege. The few safe shelters—shallow tunnels and caves along the bleak chalk slopes of Monte Cassino [site of the monastery/fortress]—were exclusively for the young fanatics of the 1st Parachute Division. . . .

The uncanny stillness, broken only by the rumble of bulldozers wrestling with drifted rubble, intensified rather than lightened the uncompromising grimness of the scene. From the desolate cathedral on the southern outskirts of Cassino we looked across stagnant pools of water to where the ruined shops and houses rose tier on tier against the steep bare slopes of Abbey Hill. The terraced olive orchards rising almost to the monastery were reduced to successive levels of blackened stumps. Not one flower, not one blade of grass, lived in the gardens of the town."

After the overthrow of the Fascist government, an elderly woman casts the first vote of her life in the Italian election of March 1946. Never before in the nation's history had women been allowed to vote.

tutional assembly were selected. Women voted for the first time in this election. The Christian Democrats won 31 percent of the vote, with the Socialists getting 20 percent and the Communists 19 percent. On the same day, people had the chance to decide on whether the country was to remain a monarchy or become a republic. Victor Emmanuel III had abdicated in favor of his son, Umberto II. However, the people voted 12.7 million to 10.7 million in favor of the republic. Umberto left the country.

The constitution was debated for two years. Although the Socialists and Communists theoretically could have dominated, they were badly split on policy matters. Also, as the United States and the Soviet Union became enemies in the cold war, the Italians had differing views about whether to side with Western Europe and the Americans or Eastern Europe and the Soviet Union.

The new form of government was almost like the parliamentary system under the old monarchy except that now the head of the nation was the president, elected by the parliament for a seven-year term. The real power lay with the Council of Ministers, headed by the prime minister, and the legislature, consisting of the Chamber of Deputies and the Senate. The legislators were elected so that representation was proportional to the population. Judges were independent but subject to the Supreme Council of the Judiciary. Cases could be taken to the Constitutional Court, and citizens could challenge laws by taking steps to put unwanted laws to a vote (a referendum). Regional governments were set up. The agreements of the 1929 Lateran Pact with the Vatican were made part of the nation's law. In addition, the constitution spoke of rights to employment, free education, a living wage, free health care, and profit sharing. Big landholdings were to be broken up and redistributed.

THE ITALIAN ECONOMIC MIRACLE

Economic growth under the new republic was spectacular. At first American support helped to rebuild the basic industries. All the Italian factions cooperated to get reconstruction under way. By 1948, the country's factories had reached prewar production levels. Until 1964, industry grew at the rate of 8 percent a year.

Italy was one of the founding members of the European Economic Community, established by the Treaties of Rome in 1957. The goal was to remove trade barriers so that products and labor might move more easily among the European nations.

ECONOMIC PROBLEMS

In 1963 the trade unions became very powerful in Italy, obtaining higher wages for their members and higher prices for everybody. Workers held unofficial strikes and mass demonstrations. Jobs were practically guaranteed. Businesses—especially in the textile and light engineering industries—switched to piecework with off-the-books workers who could be dismissed and were not entitled to a guaranteed wage. Unemployment hit young people hard. By 1977 a million Italians under age twenty-four were unemployed. The currency, the lira, dropped in value with respect to the U.S. dollar. But there was another period of economic growth in the mid-1980s as inflation slowed and national income per person overtook that of Britain.

Land reforms in the 1950s called for the state to take over large, poorly farmed pieces of land. The idea was to improve the land and sell it to new owners who had been tenants or even servants before. Very few families actually acquired land in this way, however. Rather, the people without land drifted to the cities or left Italy. The government officials who ran the redistribution program, by virtue of their control of the land, weakened the power traditionally held by families.

In 1950 the people in the south were averaging half the income of northern Italians. To correct the imbalance, the Southern Development Fund was set up. Few new industries were established, though the south benefited from better roads, health services, and schools, and improved availability of water. Also, change came to the south as people became accustomed to using automobiles, watching

ITALY AND THE EUROPEAN UNION

Plans for establishing a trading area, called a common market, for Western Europe were discussed by nations in 1955 at a meeting in Messina, Sicily. This idea was formalized in the Treaties of Rome in 1957 with the creation of the European Economic Community (EEC). Italy was one of the original members, along with France, Belgium, Luxembourg, the Netherlands, and West Germany.

In 1967 the EEC joined with other international committees dealing with coal and steel and with atomic energy to form the European Communities, which became known as the European Community in the 1980s and the European Union in 1991. The real power in this organization lies with the Council of Ministers, made up of one representative from each of the member nations. There is also a European Parliament, which is a legislative body, a European Court of Justice, which is the judicial branch, a European Investment Bank, which guarantees loans for government projects, and an Economic and Social Committee that can be consulted on policy.

One of the goals of the Union is to establish a single currency regulated by one central bank. For such a scheme to work without forcing the debts of some nations to be shared by countries with stronger economies or more disciplined spending practices, all member countries must meet strict standards. Because of Italy's economic problems in the early 1990s, the lira was temporarily forced out of the European Monetary System. The Italian government responded with efforts to reduce the budget deficit and cut back on spending. By 1998 Italy was included in the first group of European Union countries that were to do away with their traditional monetary systems in favor of the new currency, the Euro.

television, and having access to processed food. The young left the south, and although many sent part of their wages back to their families, some rural areas were nearly depopulated. This trend in emigration was reversed by the 1980s. One notable business success in the south was the achievement of control of the world's heroin trade in the mid-1980s by the Mafia. The gangster group also had other illegal means of creating wealth for its top-ranking officers and for the trusted workers who carried out day-to-day criminal activities.

CHANGES IN SOCIETY

A tobacco farmer harvests his crop in southeast Italy. Despite land reforms made in the 1950s to increase productivity and turn acreage over to former tenants and servants, many southerners left the area for the big cities or America.

After World War II, Italy had the lowest birthrate of any industrial country. A partial explanation for this downward trend may be found in the use of abortion and contraceptives and the availability of the option of divorce. Family law began to change. Divorce was made legal in 1970 and confirmed by referendum in 1974 by 59.1 percent of the voters. Abortion was legalized in a 1978 law that received a 67.9 percent vote of approval when it was put to a public vote in 1981. By 1979, almost 12 percent of the marriages were civil—not

involving a religious ceremony. Education of girls in the secondary schools became widespread only in the 1960s. Now, with education, women could secure paying jobs outside the home.

These changes show that Italy was becoming more of a secular society—that is, less heavily influenced by religion. Regular attendance at church is estimated to have dropped from about 70 percent in the mid-1950s to 30 percent in the 1980s. A new agreement was reached in 1984 between the Vatican and the Italian government under which Roman Catholicism ceased to be the state religion, religious instruction in schools became voluntary, and the state stopped funding the salaries of priests.

An increase in violence and bribery has posed other challenges for the Italians. In 1969 a series of bombings and train derailments shocked the nation. These acts of terrorism were carried out by right-wing groups called neofascist because they openly adopted many of the worst policies of Mussolini. Their idea was to attack the gangs of labor and perhaps provoke an overthrow of the government. Then by the mid-1970s, young left-wingers began to use terrorism to protest the international policies of the United States. In 1978 a group of students and workers called the Red Brigades kidnapped and murdered Aldo Moro, a former prime minister. With increased police power and court trials of the terrorists, the threat of violence was greatly reduced by 1981–1982.

Then in 1992 a scandal about bribes given to and solicited by public officials broke. It started in Milan when an investigation uncovered so much evidence of wrongdoing that the city became known as "Bribesville." Dozens of leading politicians, government officials, and businessmen were arrested and imprisoned for their participation in illegal deals.

OTHER CRISES

Many of the problems Italy is facing as the country moves to the twenty-first century are familiar ones—divisions within the country, presence of new immigrant groups, and difficulties associated with international trade. Unity or division of the country is still an issue. One group, the Northern League, which secured about 20 percent of the northern vote in 1992, pushed for a new constitution in which Italy would be divided into three separate republics that would be subject to a common government only in matters of defense, foreign affairs, and monetary policy.

Immigration and labor supply is another problem. Foreigners flock to Italy when labor is in short supply in Italian industry or when political turmoil forces them to leave their own countries. There are now some seven hundred thousand Muslims in Italy. They represent the second largest religious group after Roman Catholics. Many Italians who hold to the traditional values of their ancient land have had difficulty in accepting some people from other cultures.

International developments have also resulted in changes. With the collapse of the Soviet Union, the Communist Party lost strength. Italy's role in the European Union means pressure for stricter financial policies. A program of returning state-run businesses to private hands was begun. As the European countries come together for trade and monetary purposes, tensions have developed with the European Union. Yet progress has been made in establishing a single European currency, and Italy plans to participate in the coming changeover. As a result, the Euro (European Union currency) eventually will replace the lira as legal tender in Italy.

INTO THE FUTURE

In the twentieth century, Italy was involved in two world wars and tried three forms of government: monarchy, dictatorship, and republic. The country's recovery from the devastation of World War II was remarkable. Democratic institutions have been reinstated, economic gains have been made, and Italy is playing an important role in the development of the European Union.

ACHIEVEMENTS OF ITALIANS

5

The creativity of Italians is expressed in many ways in religion, the arts, in science, and in industrial design. The works of present-day Italians enrich the lives of their fellow countrymen and also the culture of the world.

THE ROLE OF ITALIANS IN THE ROMAN CATHOLIC CHURCH

Italians have traditionally dominated the Papacy, the system of government of the Roman Catholic Church. When Polish-born Karol Wojtyla was installed as Pope John Paul II in 1978, he was the first non-Italian to hold that position in 456 years. Italians have been among the best and the worst of the popes. For example, Angelo Giuseppe Roncalli, who was Pope John XXIII from 1958 to 1963, is esteemed as one of the great reformers of the church. Italians have accounted for a disproportionate share of the saints of the church—an imbalance that is only now being adjusted as recent popes have acknowledged the achievements of people of other nations.

Italian society is overwhelmingly Catholic, and many of the private schools are run by the church, but Italians are often hostile to or ambivalent about the clergy and about the church as an institution. Franco Ferrarotti, an Italian professor of sociology, explains:

Institutionally speaking, religion has never been taken seriously. Italians have always been Catholics and atheists at the same time. Religion is not an issue in this country. It is the only country in Europe where religion is not a popular issue. Once Pope Pius IX had defined papal infallibility [in 1870] there was no room for discussion any more. Italians are very practical people. If the Pope is infallible they said to themselves, why waste time in discussion, let's forget about it.[13]

A MODERN ITALIAN'S TESTIMONY ABOUT HIS FAITH

Ferruccio Berolo, born and baptized at Belluno in the foothills of the Alps, describes his feelings about his parish church in *Italians,* by David Willey (London: British Broadcasting Corporation, 1984) at p. 139:

"I was brought up as a Catholic like everyone else in my generation, but I don't go to Mass very often. The church, and religion, for me is the moment when I feel I must sit down and rest, not just my body, but my soul.

"I am particularly fond of the church in Belluno where all my family was baptised and married, and where they started their journey toward eternity. Apart from the beauty of that church, it gives you the sense that life is rather like standing on a bridge. If you look in one direction, you just see life going past, and that's a bit sad. But if you turn your head the other way, you see the water all alive rushing toward you.

"Going into that church I understand that life really has such a marvelous continuity, that this is the place where my life started, and that of my ancestors, and where their lives stopped and where, probably, I hope, my own life will stop. That gives you a sense of peace and quiet. Everything seems to settle down into its proper place. You feel you belong to a much bigger dimension, and that feeling gives me an immense sense of peace."

THE ROLE OF ROMAN CATHOLICISM
IN THE LIVES OF ITALIANS

The Roman Catholic Church has influence on the lives of the 80 percent of Italians estimated to be members. Even many Italians allied with the Communist Party send their children to church on Sunday. However, Italians voted against following church teachings on questions such as divorce and abortion. These votes are another signal of the decline in the influence of the church.

Many Italian Roman Catholics take their faith and churches in their towns for granted. Frances Mayes, an American, makes the following observation about how some Italians relate to the church:

We arrive as vespers [evening prayers] begin. Only a dozen people are here and three of these are women fanning themselves and chatting just behind us. Usually, the habit of regarding the church as an extension of the living room or piazza charms me, but today I turn and stare at them because the five Augustinian monks who strode in and took up their books have begun the Gregorian chant of this hour. . . . But the women are unmoved; perhaps they come every day. In the middle, they saunter noisily out, all three talking at once.[14]

Despite the weakening influence of Roman Catholicism, for many Italians it remains a valued link to the past and a way of expressing present needs. Pilgrimages are especially important in the south, where thousands will follow a trail each year to one of the major shrines. Statues of saints are paraded through the town squares. Feast days are observed. The ties to the local church, scene of so many family baptisms, weddings, and funerals, are strong.

MUSIC

It is not just Gregorian chants that Italians have contributed to music. Indeed, the system of musical notation was developed by a monk, Guido d'Arezzo, who lived around 995–1050. Antonio Stradivari (1644–1737) crafted violins that are prized today. Italian composers such as Claudio Monteverdi, Antonio Vivaldi, Gioacchino Rossini, and Giuseppe Verdi have contributed greatly to the fields of opera, church music, and chamber music.

Italians love opera, and almost every large city has a theater devoted to live presentations of these musical dramas. One of the most famous opera houses in the world is La Scala, in Milan. Opera began in the late sixteenth century as an attraction at the weddings of wealthy Italian families, and Italian composers have continued to furnish new ideas for this art form.

The golden age of Italian opera included the masterpieces of Vincenzo Bellini, Gaetano Donizetti, Verdi, and Giacomo Puccini. However, contemporary composer Luciano Berio has created a form of music theater that takes traditional opera in new directions. Moreover, many of the great singers of all time have been Italian. The gifted tenor Luciano Pavarotti has done much to popularize opera with the general public and has also worked with groups performing nonoperatic music. He represents a line of brilliant performers going back to Enrico Caruso.

FESTIVAL AND DANCE

Festivals featuring classical, jazz, and popular music are held regularly in Italian cities. For example, the world-famous Festival of Two Worlds celebrates music, as well as drama and dance, every year in Spoleto.

The list of festivals in the many cities of Italy is almost endless. Venice has its boat races. San Miniato, in Tuscany, flies kites. Florence has an exploding carriage and fireworks. Streets carpeted with flower pictures are featured in Genzano, south of Rome. Rome has a race of horse-drawn carriages. In Marostica, the town square is turned into a giant chessboard with costumed humans taking the role of the chess pieces.

Many of these festivals provide the opportunity to see what people wore at different times in history. One of the most famous is the Palio, in Siena. Twice a year, there is a bareback horse race in which riders compete for a silk banner called the palio. The first recorded race dates back to 1238, but the event may go back to Roman military training.

Some of the festivals are devoted to dance. One famous Italian folk dance the tarantella, is said to have originated in the fifteenth or seventeenth century around the southern city of Taranto. People thought they could cure the bite of a tarantula by dancing hard enough to sweat the spider's poison from their system.

LUCIANO PAVAROTTI

Born in 1935 in Modena, Italy, Pavarotti is noted for being able to reach the highest notes of the range in which a tenor sings. He often sings on television. One of the most popular performances has been "Three Tenors" in which he has shared the stage with Placido Domingo and Jose Carrera. He also has performed popular music.

Pavarotti graduated from a teaching institute in Modena and taught elementary school for two years. He studied voice privately. After winning a singing competition, the Concorso Internationale, he first sang opera professionally in Reggio Emilia, Italy. He then sang in opera houses in Europe and Australia. His debut at the Metropolitan Opera in New York City, in 1968, was a smashing success. Since then, he has performed frequently in the world's most prestigious opera houses.

Luciano Pavarotti greets his fans with open arms before a performance.

Movies

With so much practice in the production of local festivals, perhaps it is not surprising that Italy is home to a thriving motion picture industry. Italian films are an important export. Moreover, so many American films were made on Italian locations during the 1950s when European wages and costs were low that Rome was called Hollywood on the Tiber. In 1996 the Italian film *Il Postino* was nominated for the Best Picture award by Hollywood's Motion Picture Academy. The lead in that picture, Massimo Troisi, was nominated for an Oscar for Best Actor. It is unusual for Hollywood to give such recognition to a foreign film.

Federico Fellini is just one of the many great movie directors who brought international recognition to the Italian film industry during the 1950s and 1960s.

Italy has produced great film directors: Roberto Rossellini, Vittorio De Sica, Luchino Visconti, and Federico Fellini. Famous actors and actresses include Anna Magnani, Sophia Loren, Vittorio Gassman, and Marcello Mastroianni. However, the Italian style of making pictures differs from the American. The American actress Ingrid Bergman was amazed when she worked for Rossellini and was given no production schedule. Mastroianni reported the same lack of regimentation with Fellini a generation later: "I show up at the set in the morning, and ask Fellini, 'Hey Feder'i, what do you want me to do today?' "[15]

A spin-off from the movie industry is the word "paparazzi," used to denote the freelance photographers who try aggressively for candid shots of famous people. Appropriately enough, the origin of the term is embedded in an Italian movie, *La Dolce Vita.* Filmmaker Fellini called a photographer character in that movie Paparazzo, and the name stuck.

Painting and Sculpture

Italy's great tradition of painters dating from the Renaissance has not continued into modern times. Some people explain the apparent drying up of national talent in this field by citing the foreign domination Italy experienced after the mid–sixteenth century. With the rise of Futurism in the early years of the present century, however, Umberto Boccioni and Giacomo Balla made names for themselves. Indeed, Boccioni, creator of *Unique Forms of Continuity in Space* (1913), was one of the major figures of the Futurist movement. He believed that nontraditional materials such as wood, glass, cloth, and electric lights could be used together in one piece and that sculpture can mold and enclose space within itself. Later there was Giorgio de Chirico, who influenced the Surrealists in the 1920s. More recently Giorgio Morandi's work has been appreciated. Then there is Lucio Fontana, who adopts such modern forms as a blank canvas slashed open by a knife and a room wrapped in nylon fabric.

The desire to conserve some of the greatest Western art masterpieces has fallen to Italy, where the sheer number of art works makes this a daunting task. Italy's efforts in this area have contributed to an understanding of restoration of Renaissance art. When dirt and dust have accumulated on a painting for centuries, the canvas or plaster must be cleaned very carefully so that the underlying paint is not hurt. Important masterpieces including Michelangelo's ceiling of the Sistine Chapel and Leonardo's fresco *The Last Supper* have undergone restoration.

Modern Italians have contributed many works of sculpture to grace their cities. Beginning in the 1880s Medardo Rosso experimented with new ways of using wax. He influenced other Italian sculptors such as Arturo Martini, Giacomo Manzú, Marino Marini, and Alberto Viani. Twentieth-century Italian sculptors include Alberto Burri, noted for his metal reliefs. Marini and Luciano Minguzzi have developed a bold and amply proportioned style for portraying human figures. Mirko Basaldella's war memorial gate as a monument to hostages in World War II has drawn praise.

Italy's rich heritage of fine art is carried on by an artist painting a landscape. The country has taken on the challenge of preserving some of the great masterpieces of Western art while at the same time exploring new forms of artistic expression.

ARCHITECTURE

Just as many paintings and frescoes of the Renaissance require restoration after centuries of neglect, buildings of that era have been damaged by exposure to acids in the smoke from factories. But if industrial pollution acts slowly, floods like the one that hit Venice and Florence in 1966 call for emergency action to save historic buildings and their contents. Because of the sheer volume of art treasures at risk, international help is often gladly accepted.

In architecture, Italians have a continuous record of high achievement. From the unequaled public works of the Roman Empire through the famous churches and palaces of the Renaissance, Italians have made buildings of great style. Thomas Jefferson was intrigued by the work of sixteenth-century architect Andrea Palladio, who used components of ancient Roman temples in his designs for private residences, and the third president of the United States borrowed this idea in some buildings he designed in his home state of Virginia. Thus, through Jefferson's influence on U.S. architecture, many American buildings reflect classic Italian ideas.

As for modern architecture, twice Italian architects have been honored with the Pritzker Architecture Prize, architec-

Milan Cathedral is a stunning example of Italy's achievement in the field of architecture. Milan is also the home of a revolutionary twenty-six-story tower that introduced the use of reinforced concrete in large structures.

ture's highest honor. In 1990 Aldo Rossi won; and in 1998, Renzo Piano. Rossi has recently designed two office buildings for the Walt Disney town of Celebration outside Orlando, Florida. Piano, too, is working on projects in the United States—in Cambridge, Massachusetts, for Harvard University. His conversion of the Lingotto factory in Turin and his home in Genoa show creative use of glass. Another Italian architect, Torre Velasca, designed an important building of the 1950s, a twenty-six-story tower in Milan that pioneered the use of reinforced concrete.

DESIGN

Design is an important element of architecture, but it figures everywhere in the visual and decorative arts. For example, the penmanship of Italian Renaissance scribes, who copied manuscripts before printing was invented, was so admired that a version of it is taught to first graders in Europe and America. Benvenuto Cellini was a great goldsmith of the Renaissance.

Florentine mosaics and Venetian glass are crafts that attract collectors even now.

Today, Italian designs in cars such as the Ferrari and the Fiat, motor scooters such as the Vespa, or teakettles such as the Alessi model attract attention. No longer is it necessary to be a prince or wealthy banker to afford good design.

THE VATICAN CITY-STATE

The Vatican is a separate state, surrounded by but not a part of Rome. It occupies 109 acres, and in 1996 its estimated population was 850. The chief of state is the pope, but the territory is administered by five church officials called cardinals. As a separate country, it has its own flag, telephone system, post office, radio station, newspaper, banking system, coins, stores, and pharmacy. Food, water, electric power, gas, and other essentials must be acquired from Italy and elsewhere, however.

The Vatican has its own army, the hundred-member Swiss Guard, a unit drawn from citizens of Switzerland, whose duty is to protect the pope. Their dress uniform was designed by Michelangelo. St. Peter's Basilica and the Vatican museums also attract many visitors, and religious pilgrims come from all over the world to catch a glimpse of the pope and to attend religious services.

Saint Peter's Basilica in Vatican City. Religious pilgrims gather here during holy days to receive blessings from the pope.

Italians have paid attention to the attractiveness of household things. Designers even have come up with new shapes for pasta.

Italians have made names for themselves and their country in the field of fashion design. Giorgio Armani of Milan and Valentino of Rome are important in the fashion world. Gucci's shoes carry on a long-standing Italian tradition of excellence in leather work.

LITERATURE

Italy has a strong tradition in writing, from Virgil's *Aeneid* in Roman times to Dante's *Divine Comedy* to modern Nobel Prize winners for literature, Luigi Pirandello (1934) and Dario Fo (1997). Pirandello, from Sicily, wrote *Six Characters In Search of an Author.* Fo is a playwright, manager-director, and actor. Another Italian author, Umberto Eco, wrote a popular novel called *The Name of the Rose*, which was made into a film starring Sean Connery in 1986. Carlo Collodi, whose real name was Carlo Lorenzini, is the author of *Pinocchio.* This beloved children's book, written in 1911, was turned into a movie in 1940.

Among a distinguished set of twentieth-century philosophers are Italians Benedetto Croce (1866–1952) and Antonio Gramsci (1891–1937). Gramsci, a Marxist, was put in prison because of his opposition to Mussolini, and Croce, too, was well known for his anti-Fascist beliefs.

A window-shopper admires the latest in Italian fashions. Clothing and footwear from the houses of Armani and Gucci have made these designers famous for style and innovation.

SCIENCE AND INVENTIONS

The Italian tradition in science can be traced from Archimedes (born around 287 B.C. in Sicily), who formulated the idea of specific gravity, through Pliny the Elder, who cataloged his knowledge in *Natural History* in 77 A.D., to Galileo Gallilei (1564–1642), who is known for his use of the telescope and for asserting that the earth revolves around the sun. All-round

Renaissance genius Leonardo da Vinci thought up a design for a flying machine in about 1488.

In modern times, too, Italians have contributed to the world's knowledge. Luigi Galvani (1737–1798) investigated electricity in animal tissue. Alessandro Volta (1745–1827) invented the electric battery and demonstrated it for Napoleon in 1801. Guglielmo Marconi (1874–1937) invented the telegraph, a system of sending radio signals great distances. He won the Nobel Prize in physics in 1909. Enrico Fermi (1901–1954) won the Nobel Prize in physics in 1938. He was given permission by the Fascists to travel to Sweden to get the award, but he and his wife, who was Jewish, went to the United States instead of returning to Italy. Fermi directed the first controlled nuclear chain reaction and later built the first nuclear reactor, at the University of Chicago.

Rita Levi-Montalcini has done outstanding work in the field of biology. In 1986 she shared the Nobel Prize in physiology (1986) with Stanley Cohen. Levi-Montalcini, who is Jewish, had to go into hiding in Florence during World War II to escape deportation. She holds dual citizenship in Italy and the United States.

It is not unusual for a country that excels in one area of creativity to borrow heavily from other nations to round out its culture. What is so amazing about Italy is the many areas—religion, music, movies, art, architecture, design, literature, and science—to which its citizens have contributed.

Best known for his book The Name of the Rose, *author Umberto Eco is also a noted philosopher, historian, and literary critic.*

Daily Life in
Modern Italy

6

The gaiety and fun that Italians express and the security of close family connections have made daily life in modern Italy attractive. Food, festivals, and sports are important to Italians. The family is at the heart of many Italian customs. Often businesses—even large ones—are run by families. When those businesses are illegal, as in the case of the Mafia, the close-knit family structure makes law enforcement difficult.

Mamma Mia

While families are important in all cultures, the closeness of ties and the ways of expressing affection can differ greatly. In Italy, the mother–son bond is especially strong. When American and Italian troops were involved in peacekeeping operations in Somalia in 1993, Matt Frei of the British Broadcasting Corporation reported that American television showed U.S. troops going ashore from the landing craft. Italian television, however, "showed Italian soldiers bidding farewell to their mothers at the airport. Mother and soldier were crying into each other's arms. Men bristling with automatic machine guns, bayonets, and pistols were screaming 'Mamma!' No one was embarrassed." [16]

Although this mother–son bond is strong in many of the cultures that exist in the Mediterranean area, in Italy this relationship colors many aspects of life. Paul Hofmann, who for many years was chief of the *New York Times* Rome bureau, reports: "The classic Italian *mamma* pampers her boy, keeps telling him he is unique, defends him like a lioness, condones his failures and vices, schemes to get him ahead in school and in life, wants him to stay close to her if not in her home, and when he gets married is jealous of her daughter-in-law." [17]

The father–daughter tie also is close, although it is expected that when a daughter marries, she will become a part

An Italian couple on their wedding day. According to tradition, the bride will become part of her new husband's family.

of her husband's family. In traditional Italian culture, the family plays a great role in selecting the marriage partners for sons and daughters. Girls are protected by the family from acquiring a bad reputation to such an extent that it is difficult for the couples to become acquainted on dates. Traditional marriages are more common in the conservative southern part of Italy, but even there, women have more to say in marriage decisions than was true only a generation or two ago.

In 1984, David Willey, a reporter for the British Broadcasting Corporation, interviewed an Italian bride, Fortunata Manglaviti, who described her courtship in the traditional manner of a southern village as follows:

It's very difficult here to get to know your fiancé well before you marry. You can literally never be alone together. Here, the bridegroom is allowed to do what he likes, but the bride has to remain chaste and pure. If she were to go with her fiancé, this purity might not exist any longer.

When you leave school, there's almost an obligation to get married. But I suppose if you don't find the ideal man you can wait. There's no entertainment or possibility of work in the village. Staying in the house all day you feel the need to get away, have your own home and children.[18]

Now with more occupations open to women and with the possibility of escape to a city, young women have more choices. However, in cities, dating remains a problem because of space. Families are likely to take over whole apartment buildings, with the younger generations living on the top floors so that older family members have fewer stairs to climb. To have privacy on a date, a couple has to go out.

FAMILY ATTITUDES

Attitudes toward family and sex are changing. Before the era of divorce, a fair number of Italians entered into extramarital affairs. When divorce was made legal, some Italians were pressured to choose between their spouse or their other partners. Even though the divorce rate in Italy has increased, it is a comparatively low rate, at 8 percent, in comparison to one in three failed marriages in France and Britain. The low figure is less a measure of happiness than an indication of tolerance for extramarital affairs and a recognition of the importance of family identity. By 1979 almost 12 percent of all weddings took place in a city hall rather than a church, and couples living together without getting married had become more common. The number of marriages has declined from over 440,000 in 1947 to just over 300,000 in 1992.

In particular, the decade of the 1970s saw many changes. Contraception was readily available after 1971. Divorce and abortion laws were adopted. Most Italians were now living in apartments in cities rather than rural villages, and no longer needed large numbers of children to do farm chores. By 1987 Italy had the lowest birthrate of any industrial country. The south was producing so many more children than the north that some worried that the makeup of the future population of the nation would reflect the more conservative values of the south.

BAMBINI

The low birthrate does not mean that children are not prized in Italy. Indeed, the high cost of spoiling children may have led many families to limit the number of babies. According to Matt Frei:

A father and his daughter look out the window of their home. In Italy, children, or bambini, *are revered and given much affection.*

> The birth of a child is still a reason for great, albeit increasingly rare, festivities. The day a *bambino* or *bambina* is born, his or her birth is announced by a rosette pinned to the front door of the facade of the building: blue for boys, pink for girls. A British or American family looks mortified when its baby starts to scream or squeal in a restaurant or museum. In Italy it is still music to people's ears. Rich or poor, the *bambino* remains king.[19]

From ages six to eleven, Italian children are required to attend elementary school, followed by middle school for three more years. This amount of schooling has been mandated since 1948, but only since 1962 has the country enforced its compulsory education laws. The next level of schooling includes a number of options from college preparatory courses to vocational and technical institutes. There is great variation in the quality of education at the university level. In 1969, all high school graduates were declared eligible to go to university. Perhaps unsurprisingly, many students who would have had great difficulty passing a standard entrance exam flocked to the university, causing a temporary decline in standards. Because of the number of students attending, classes were huge, and library and laboratory space was limited. Since the mid-1980s, requirements have been tightened so the degrees awarded from Italian universities have more weight.

FAMILY BUSINESS AND ARRANGEMENTS

While families may want their children to be well educated, they also expect them to participate in family businesses, which can be run more cheaply if all the relatives work together. As many as 90 percent of Italian private enterprises are run by families, and some family businesses have attained international status. Such is the case of the fashion family, the Benettons of Treviso, near Venice. Luciano Benetton had training in selling clothing. His sister, Giuliana, who had been hand-knitting sweaters for herself and her brothers, learned how to use knitting machines. In 1954 the brother and sister bought a machine on credit and started turning out sweaters that the family sold. Now Benetton is the world's largest buyer of wool. The company has more than 7,000 retail stores in 120 countries. Many families dream of success on the scale of the Benetton venture. Most family businesses remain small, however.

Many businesses in Italy operate on the basis of exchanging favors—giving away valuable items or services, or providing them at greatly reduced rates. These favors or "arrangements" often are not reported for tax purposes, so they represent a "submerged" or "black" part of the economy that is not shown in official statistics. Some estimates put this "submerged" part as high as 15 percent of the total economy. Other estimates say that if illegal activities such as the drug trade are counted, the figure would be closer to 30 percent.

Anyone doing business in Italy must master the art of "the arrangement." In a very simple arrangement, a busy person might offer someone a bottle of wine to stand in line to pay a bill or to cash a check. More complex maneuvering is entailed in potentially profitable ventures like making a movie. Thus a film director may cast the girlfriend of the man putting up the money, and promise other favors to ensure the use of a coveted set. Observers of Italian life, such as Paul Hofmann, have reported that the successful arranger knows how to be indirect.

> For centuries the people had to humor local princelings. . . . To get what one wanted or avoid what one feared, one had to act by indirection, to dissemble, to play a double or triple game. Cunning as a strategy for getting on in life has been cultivated in Italy since time immemorial and is being used today in politics, business and the professions, and everyday existence.[20]

KIDNAPPING, INC., AND THE MAFIA

A more sinister form of the arrangement consists of obtaining money and power by means of murder and kidnapping. Italy has long held the European record for kidnapping complaints. Some years the count is as high as 150 to 170, excluding cases of people abducted for revenge rather than for money. For-profit kidnapping is carried out by gangs of professional criminals. This activity is centered on the island of Sardinia and in the region of Calabria, at the toe of the boot. Relatives of wealthy persons are seized and held for ransom. Often an ear or a finger cut from the person being held is sent to the relatives, to encourage them to find the money. Sometimes the victims are released after payment of the ransom, sometimes, not.

The big money, however, is made by the Mafia. This organization began in Sicily in the Middle Ages. Today, it controls the drug trade, has access to big government contracts for public works, and routinely requires legitimate businesses to pay money for "protection" against unwanted consequences such as arson and vandalism. This form of blackmail is called extortion. Although most Italians are law-abiding citizens, family ties and distrust of the police have given great power to Mafia leaders.

THE MAFIA'S CODE OF SILENCE

In Sicily, so often ruled by foreign conquerors, landowners once had small private armies to protect their estates. During the eighteenth and nineteenth centuries, these armies turned against their employers and seized power, thereafter handing out their own form of justice. Since the landlords had often been oppressive, the people accepted the new system, which limited any appeal to official law enforcement agencies. When someone was killed or otherwise wronged, it was up to the victim or the family to take revenge. To report the problem to the authorities would be to break the code of silence, which was an offense punishable by death.

An example given by Paul Hofmann in *That Fine Italian Hand* illustrates that the code of silence is still observed: "The wife of a reputed . . . informer took her dying husband to the hospital telling the nurse he was 'not feeling so good.' The postmortem found ninety bullets in his body. When police questioned the widow about who had attacked her husband, she seemed astonished: 'Did they shoot him? I didn't notice anything.' Even children will not talk."

The Italian government has been trying to eliminate the Mafia since 1871. Decades later, Mussolini boasted that he had done away with the Sicilian Mafia. However, the organization was stronger than ever after World War II. The government tried again in 1988 and 1992, in response to a series of murders whose victims included a judge and lawyers prosecuting cases against Mafia leaders. Some of the Mafia leaders were sent to prison. Leoluca Orland, an anti-Mafia mayor of Palermo, the capital of Sicily, was elected in 1993 with 75 percent of the vote showing that residents of Palermo no longer supported the Mafia. Orlando admits that the Mafia may not have been defeated, but he can point to a drop in the murder rate. Tom Hundley, correspondent for the *Chicago Tribune*, reported in April 1998: "In the 1980s, Palermo averaged about 130 murders a year. Since the beginning of 1997, there have been fewer than 10."[21]

SPORTS AND RECREATION

Italian loyalty to family, group, city, or nation finds expression in sport. Italians are enthusiastic backers of local teams in competition with each other and of national teams in competition with foreigners. Their desire to achieve has resulted in excellence in performance. They hold many medals in the Olympic Games.

Soccer (called football in Europe) is the most popular sport—whether it is a pickup game in the town square or a professional team in a World Cup match. In 1982 the Italians won the World Cup, indicating that they were the best team in the world. All Italy turned out to celebrate. When the Italian team won third place in 1990, it seemed that everyone stayed at home to watch the match on television. In 1995 Brazil defeated Italy for the World Cup by only one point. Italy played France to a tie in the 1998 quarterfinals of the World Cup but lost on penalty kicks. Not only the national contests but also local teams receive strong support from the towns and cities they represent. In Naples, a city with many poor neighborhoods, the Napoli Soccer Club easily raised several million dollars to attract players from other countries so that Naples has a better chance of beating its rivals in northern Italy.

Italians love racing of all types. Bicycle racing in the Tour of Italy each spring draws television coverage. Motorcycle racing also is popular. But it is in Formula 1, high-speed automobile racing that Italians have excelled for so long. Italy provides some of the best drivers and the best Ferrari racing machines. Some claim that the Italians take their love of racing to the highways at all times, making any driving in this country a sport.

However, there are more leisurely activities. The tradition of the Sunday walk, the *passeggiata*, is still observed. In the small towns in particular, almost everyone takes to the streets for a few hours in the afternoon. Hiking in the mountains is also popular. A game similar to bowling, *bocce*, has many followers.

Formula 1 racers battle for first place in the Italian Grand Prix. Drivers often use similar tactics on Italy's roadways.

VACATIONS AND FESTIVALS

August is the vacation month in Italy, and many restaurants, stores, and factories close down for at least two weeks. While the number of Italians who travel abroad is increasing, the majority still vacation in Italy at the seaside or in the mountains.

Given the predominance of the Roman Catholic church, the biggest festivals revolve around important religious events and symbols. Christmas is celebrated with special foods depending on the locality. The Christmas cake, called *panettone*, is a light sponge cake with candied fruit and raisins. However, children do not receive their presents until Epiphany or Twelfth Night, January 6. Instead of Santa Claus, Italian children look forward to the arrival of the Befana, an old peasant woman who rides a donkey, climbs down chimneys, and leaves treats. The children put out some supper for Befana and a carrot or apple for her donkey.

The day before the beginning of Lent is called Carnival Day. As on Mardi Gras in New Orleans, people dress up in fancy clothes, often with spectacular masks. They go to parties, play practical jokes, and indulge in food they will refrain from eating during Lent, the penitential season that precedes Easter. On Easter, the Italians again celebrate with special food. Lamb is a favorite meat, but each district has its traditional dish. In the south, it may be a pastry with eggs and ham. In Liguria, in the northwest, there is a pie made with 33 thin sheets of pastry (symbolizing the years in the life of Jesus) filled with cheese, eggs, and spinach.

A festivalgoer shows off his costume on Carnival Day, a celebration held just before the beginning of Lent.

Children in Sicily look forward to November and All Saints' Day, followed by All Souls' Day, when the dead are said to depart from the cemeteries and leave presents for children who have been good. Besides toys, children receive objects made of marzipan, an almond paste that is good to eat. The paste can be colored and shaped to look like almost anything. One mother reports: "Today it is still possible to play a practical joke with *pasta reale*, . . . you can buy cakes

TRAFFIC AND WHAT IT SAYS ABOUT ITALIANS

When American professor Frances Mayes moved to Italy, she learned about the speed and daredevil tactics of Italian drivers. In *Under the Tuscan Sun*, Mayes describes Italian driving and her American male companion's reaction:

> Most travellers here feel that driving in Rome qualifies as an experience that can be added to one's *vita* [resumé] that everyday *autostrada* [freeway] trips are examinations in courage and that the Amalfi coast drive is a definition of hell. "These people really know how to drive," I remember [my friend] saying as he swung our no-power rented Fiat into the passing lane, turn signal blinking. A Maserati zooming forward in the rearview mirror blasted us back to the right lane. Soon he was admiring daring maneuvers. "Did you see *that?* He had two wheels dangling in thin air!" he marveled. "Sure, they have their share of duffers riding the center lane but most people keep to the rules."
>
> "What rules?" I asked as someone in a tiny car like ours whizzed by going a hundred. Apparently there *are* speed limits, according to the size of the engine, but I never have seen anyone stopped for speeding in all my summers in Italy. You're dangerous if you're going sixty. I'm not sure what the accident rate is; I rarely see one but I imagine many are caused by slow drivers (tourists perhaps?) who incite the cars behind them.
>
> In Naples, Mayes and her companion saw cars driving on the sidewalk while pedestrians filled the streets. Naples has a reputation for being one of the worst cities on earth for drivers and no one tries to hide it. Mayes describes comments from the mayor of Naples about driving habits in his city. "A green light is a green light, *avanti, avanti.* . . . A red light—just a suggestion. . . . Yellow is for gaiety."

of soap, sandwiches with the filling dribbling out, even complete meals served on paper plates. I once gave my children fried eggs and peas for supper, and it wasn't until they put their forks to it that they realized it was made of marzipan."[22]

FOOD

In a culture centered on the family, food naturally occupies a place of great importance. Breakfast may be only a quick snack of bread and hot chocolate or a milky coffee, called cappuccino. But with a long lunch break—sometimes two hours—many people go home to eat. Since they have not eaten much since the night before, they are hungry and dig into pasta, which is very filling. The big meal is eaten around 7 P.M. and might include vegetable soup, bread, meat, salad, and wine, followed by fruit. Then at night many Italians go for a stroll and gather to enjoy strong black coffee, called espresso, or ice cream at counters or restaurants. Some of the big cities, such as Milan, now have American fast-food restaurants that are attracting teenagers.

Italians shop daily for fresh food. Italy has many more small grocery stores than large supermarkets. Some towns hold open-air markets once a week to allow residents to buy fruit, vegetables, cheeses, and meats directly from the farms. Traditionally, meat was rarely served, but with greater wealth in the country, it is becoming more common. Kitchens are simpler in Italy than in many countries with fewer homes having freezers or microwave ovens.

Italian food is very popular throughout the world. It is considered to be one of the world's great cuisines. Also the Mediterranean diet, with starches such as bread, pasta, and potatoes, together with fruit, vegetables, olive oil, and fish, has been found to be healthy—less likely to contribute to heart disease or diabetes than the foods low in fiber and high in unhealthy fats that are prevalent in much of the developed world. The worldwide popularity of pasta and pizza may be the result of Italians emigrating to so many other countries during the nineteenth and twentieth centuries.

A butcher prepares his wares for sale in an open-air market. Once considered a luxury, meat is becoming more common as Italy's economy prospers.

TALKING

While Italian is the national language, often the dialects, or versions that are spoken in different areas, sound so

PASTA AND PIZZA

Nothing demonstrates the many traditions that exist in Italy quite so well as the variations in pasta and pizza. Pasta is the national dish of Italy, served at least once a day and sometimes twice. One way of helping a poor friend or relative is expressed in the saying: "There will always be a plate of pasta for you in my house."

The variation in pastas is described by Paul Hofmann in *That Fine Italian Hand:*

> Each region has developed its own specialties: ravioli in the North, lasagne in "fat" Bologna, papardelle with venison-based sauce in Tuscany, tortellini in Latium, macaroni and linguine in Naples, cannelloni in Sicily. Trimmings and seasonings range from greenish pesto— finely chopped basil, other herbs, and garlic mixed with cheese and pine nuts—in Genoa to clams in Naples and eggplant in Palermo. The town of Amatrice, just northeast of Rome is famous for its *spaghetti all'amatriciana*, with bacon and pepper. . . . Orthodox eaters will nevertheless request their spaghetti served just with fresh tomato pulp, the basic Neapolitan recipe.

Pizza, so popular across the world, has ancient beginnings. According to Elizabeth Romer in *Italian Pizza and Hearth Breads:*

> The story behind pizza is far older than even the crumbling walls of ancient Rome. From anonymous Neolithic people to my present Tuscan neighbors, people have baked simple hearthbreads . . . on hot stones, clay discs and, later, metal bakestones specially prepared for the purpose; and being pleased by variety they have seasoned them with whatever good things there were at hand. These simple breads are the forerunners of pizza.

The first pizzeria opened in Naples around 1830. The version of pizza in this city is a flat disk of dough topped with olive oil, tomatoes, and mozzarella cheese. Roman pizza has no tomatoes but uses onion and olives, in Liguria in northwest Italy, pizza ingredients traditionally include olives, onions, and anchovies.

The popularity of pizza migrated to the United States with the Italian community in New York City where the first pizzeria appeared in 1905. However, the food did not really catch on in America until after World War II.

different from each other that one Italian may not understand what a fellow citizen is saying. Now with television, a more standardized language may emerge. Even so, there remain small areas of Italy where French, German, Albanian, or Arabic is spoken.

Body language and hand gestures accompany every conversation in Italian. Italians seem unable to communicate with words alone. Frances Mayes, an American who bought a home in Tuscany, reports: "I saw a man step outside the confining telephone booth so he could wave his hands while talking. Many people pull over to the side of the road to talk on their car phones because they simply cannot keep a hand on the wheel, one on the telephone, and talk at the same time."[23]

Another common characteristic of an Italian conversation is simultaneous speaking. Even in groups of three and four, everyone seems to be talking at the same time.

STANDARD OF LIVING AND POPULATIONS SHIFTS

When economic times were hard, Italians left their country to find work. Now the prospect of jobs attracts immigrants to Italy. When industry boomed in the northern part of the nation, farmers left their land in the south to find work in factories. With the economic miracle of the 1960s, over 1.5 million people flocked to Italy from impoverished regions of Africa and Asia. Many of these immigrants entered the submerged or black economy working for low wages. Some, who were not legal immigrants, became involved in the criminal activities of the south. With the decreasing birthrate of native Italians, the labor of people from other countries may be needed to support Italy's industries and agriculture. Often the immigrants take jobs that the Italians do not want.

Many Italians are not comfortable with immigrant populations of different racial backgrounds. There have been attacks on North African immigrants in the cities. In 1996, some Italians protested the crowning of a black woman, Denny Mendez, as Miss Italy. A native of the Dominican Republic, Mendez was a naturalized citizen of Italy. Italians may have a struggle in accepting a multiracial Italy and accommodating African and Asian customs.

Italy has many problems. The differences between the north and the south and between native-born and immi-

HAND SIGNALS

Just as hand signals convey meaning in a baseball game, so in some cultures hand signals communicate almost as well as the spoken word. Paul Hofmann in *That Fine Italian Hand* presents examples:

Most Italians underline what they are saying with eloquent gestures in the Mediterranean way of illustrating spoken words with the hands. Watch that manual language when some conversation takes place behind the plate-glass windows of a store or café. Even though you cannot hear what is being said and don't know whether the voices sound cordial or angry, you may be able to guess the drift of the dialogue from the play of the hands—who is persuasive and who skeptical, who wants to convey good faith (placing his hands on his chest) and who is accusing (pointing her forefinger at the other's face).

Some common Italian gestures will at first puzzle the newcomer: The thumb joined with the forefinger and middle finger while the hand is slowly shaken from a limp wrist expresses uncertainty, disbelief, or urgent inquiry. Striking the edges of one's hands together in a crosslike pattern means "I am off" or "Let's beat it!" Such manual messages probably go back to prehistory. The famous orators of antiquity reinforced the effect of their rhetoric with ample movements of their arms and hands, as prosecutors and defense counsel in southern courtrooms still do today.

grant workers create tensions in the country. Stamping out the power of criminal elements will not be easy. New definitions of family and morality may accentuate the differences between older and younger generations. The requirements of the European Union to limit deficits in the national budget will challenge social programs and those who must plan for Italy's future.

To deal with these problems, Italy has one big asset—the resourcefulness and creativity of her people. Italians have lived through turbulent times. They have demonstrated that they can come up with solutions to difficult problems in difficult times. Italians have excelled in every area of human endeavor—religion, business, art, architecture, design, writing, music, sports, and science. They have the traditions of the Roman Empire, the Renaissance, and the Risorgimento. Italy has joined the European Union, which is poised to establish Europe as a major economic power, able to hold its own in competition with wealthy North America, as well as with populous, hardworking China. The twenty-first century can be a time of opportunity for Italians.

FACTS ABOUT ITALY

THE GOVERNMENT

Official name: Republica Italiana (Italian Republic)

Form of government: republic with two legislative houses: Senate and Chamber of Deputies

Capital: Rome

Flag: green, white, and red vertical stripes

Chief of state: president

Head of government: prime minister

Other major cities: Milan, Naples, Turin, Palermo, Genoa, Bologna, Florence, Bari, Catania, Venice

PEOPLE

Population: 57,520,000 (estimated as of January 1, 1997)—much larger than California, the state of the United States with the largest population (estimated at 29,760,021 in 1990)

Literacy: total population age 15 and over literate as of 1990: 47,507,000 (97.1%)

Food: daily per capita caloric intake as of 1992: 3,561 (vegetable products 75%, animal products 25%)

LAND

Location: Southern Europe, with land extending in boot shape into the Mediterranean Sea with islands including Sicily, Sardinia, and Elba

Area: 116,324 square miles (301,277 square kilometers)—more than Arizona, less than New Mexico

Land (1994): forested 23.0%, meadows and pastures 15.4%, agricultural under permanent cultivation 37.9%; other 23.7%

INDUSTRY

Imports (1994): transport equipment 11.2%, precision machinery 5.7%, chemicals 16.3%, metal and semiprocessed metal 7.8%, food and live animals 6.7%, crude petroleum 5.1%, textiles 4.3%

Major import sources (1994): Germany 19.2%, France 13.0%, United Kingdom 6.3%, United States 4.6%, Spain 4.3%, Switzerland 3.9%

Exports (1994): transport equipment 10.7%, electrical machinery 5.1%, precision machinery 3.8%, chemicals 10.1%, textiles 8.4%, wearing apparel 7.7% (includes shoes 2.8%), metal and processed metal 6.7%

Export destinations (1994): Germany 19.0%, France 13.1%, United States 7.8%, and United Kingdom 6.5%

NOTES

CHAPTER 1: THE BOOT AND WHAT'S IN IT

1. Charles Dickens, *Pictures from Italy* (1845). New York: Coward, McCann & Geoghegan, 1973, pp. 67–68.

CHAPTER 2: FROM EARLY HUMANS TO THE END OF THE ROMAN EMPIRE

2. Quoted in Time-Life Books, eds., *The Human Dawn: Barbarian Tides.* Alexandria, VA: Time-Life Books, 1987, p. 115.

3. Quoted in Michael Grant, "The Truth About Etruscan Women," in Joseph J. Thorndike Jr., ed., *Discovery of Lost World.* New York: American Heritage, 1979, p. 173.

4. Time-Life Books, eds., *Empires Besieged.* Alexandria, VA: Time-Life Books, 1988, p. 33.

5. Time-Life Books, eds., *Rome: Echoes of Imperial Glory.* Alexandria, VA: Time-Life Books, 1994, p. 146.

CHAPTER 3: FROM THE BREAKUP OF THE EMPIRE TO REUNIFICATION

6. Quoted in Vincent Cronin, *The Horizon Concise History of Italy.* New York: American Heritage, 1972, p. 179.

7. Quoted in Cronin, *The Horizon Concise History of Italy*, p. 179.

8. Quoted in Cronin, *The Horizon Concise History of Italy*, p. 197.

CHAPTER 4: ITALY IN THE TWENTIETH CENTURY

9. Quoted in Valerio Lintner, *A Traveller's History of Italy*, 4th ed. New York: Interlink Books, 1997, p. 173.

10. Quoted in Lintner, *A Traveller's History of Italy*, p. 196.

11. Quoted in *Encyclopaedia Britannica*, "Fascism: The Italian Experience: Triumph and Decline of Italian Fascism." Compact disc edition, 1998.

12. Quoted in *Encyclopaedia Britannica*, "20th-Century International Relations: World War II, 1939–45." Compact disc edition, 1998.

CHAPTER 5: ACHIEVEMENTS OF ITALIANS

13. Quoted in David Willey, *Italians*. London: British Broadcasting Corporation, 1984, p. 135.

14. Frances Mayes, *Under the Tuscan Sun: At Home in Italy*. New York: Broadway Books, 1996, p. 162.

15. Quoted in Paul Hofmann, *That Fine Italian Hand*. New York: Henry Holt, 1990, p. 92.

CHAPTER 6: DAILY LIFE IN MODERN ITALY

16. Matt Frei, *Getting the Boot: Italy's Unfinished Revolution*. New York: Times Books, Random House, 1995, p. 106.

17. Hofmann, *That Fine Italian Hand*, p. 133.

18. Quoted in Willey, *Italians*, pp. 144–145.

19. Frei, *Getting the Boot*, pp. 109–110.

20. Hofmann, *That Fine Italian Hand*, p. 108.

21. Tom Hundley, "Anti-Mafia Sweep Helps Sicilian Capital Clean Up Its Act," *Chicago Tribune*, April 22, 1998, sec. 1, 7.

22. Mary Taylor Simeti, "On Persephone's Island," in *Italy in Mind*, Alice Leccese Powers, ed., New York: Vintage Books, Random House, 1997, p. 272.

23. Mayes, *Under the Tuscan Sun*, pp. 185–186.

CHRONOLOGY

B.C.

ca. 200,000
First human Italians (probably *Homo erectus)*

ca. 60,000
Neanderthals (early human form)

ca. 10,000
Cro-Magnons (early human form)

ca. 5000
Glacial ages ending—climate, animals, and plants close to modern types

ca. 3500–2500
Agriculture begins

ca. 3000
Ice Man lived

ca. 2000–1800
Copper use widespread

ca. 1800
Bronze use

ca. 1000–800
Iron use

ca. 800
Greek settlements in Sicily and the south

753
Traditional date for founding of Rome by Romulus

ca. 700
Beginning of Etruscan civilization

ca. 650
Etruscan expansion south

616–510
Etruscan rule in Rome

524
Battle of Cumae: Greek victory halts Etruscan expansion

509
Beginning of Roman Republic

334–264
Roman conquest and colonization of Italy

265
End of Etruscan period

264–146
Three Punic wars ending with destruction of Carthage

49–44
Julius Caesar rules as dictator

31
Augustus takes over—Roman Empire period begins

A.D.

70–235
Roman Empire at height of size and power

79
Vesuvius erupts, destroying Pompeii and Herculaneum

313
Constantine grants freedom of worship for Christians

410
Sack of Rome by Alaric

754
Pepin III (Frankish king) invades Italy

800
Charlemagne (Frankish king) becomes Holy Roman Emperor

827
Arab invasion of Sicily

900
Greatest extent of Arab power in Italy

961
German king Otto I crowned king of Italy, later Holy Roman Emperor

962
Otto I becomes Holy Roman Emperor

1072
Normans take Palermo, bringing southern Italy to control of the West

1077
German king Henry IV humiliated at Canossa

1081
Henry IV invades Italy; later is crowned Holy Roman Emperor

1250
Renaissance period begins

1309
The papacy is moved from Rome to Avignon, France

1348
The Black Death, a plague, hits Italian cities

1377
Pope Gregory XI returns the papacy to Rome from France

1455
Italian League is formed

1494
Charles VIII of France invades Italy

1530
Hapsburg ruler Charles V is crowned head of Holy Roman Empire

1633
Galileo is condemned in Rome

1713
At Peace of Utrecht, Italy given to Austrian Hapsburgs

1796
Italy is invaded by French troops, led by Napoleon Bonaparte

1815
Napoleon is defeated by European allies; Congress of Vienna divides up Italy

1848
Italians mount revolution to secure independence

1861
Victor Emmanuel II is proclaimed king; first elections for parliament of united Italy

1866
Venice becomes part of united Italy

1870
Rome is annexed to the kingdom of Italy and becomes its capital

1882
Triple Alliance of Italy with Germany and Austria–Hungary
1911–1912
Conquest of former Turkish colony of Tripoli, renamed Libya
1915
Italy enters World War I on the side of England and France
1919
Italy wins South Tyrol, but not all wanted territory, in Versailles peace talks; Mussolini organizes Fascists
1922
Mussolini is asked to become prime minister
1929
Mussolini enters into Lateran pact with the pope
1935
Ethiopian war; League of Nations sanctions
1936
Italy intervenes in Spanish Civil War; alliance with Hitler's Germany as Axis powers
1939
Italy occupies Albania
1940
Italy enters World War II on the side of Germany
1943
Allies land in Sicily; Nazis, attempting to keep Italy out of enemy hands, invade the mainland
1944
Allies take Rome
1946
Referendum rejects monarchy; republic is established
1947
Italy loses African colonies under peace settlement
1958
Italy joins the European Community (forerunner of European Union)
1959–1963
The "economic miracle"; industry grows at 8 percent a year
1966
Floods in Venice and Florence

1969

Economic crisis, bombs, and terrorism

1974

Referendum approves divorce

1981

Earthquake in Campania; referendum approves abortion

1982

Italy wins World Cup soccer contest

1985

Concordat of 1985 agreeing that Italy will have no state religion

1992

Bribery scandals in Milan; fight against Mafia and corruption increases

1993

Italian troops participate in peacekeeping operations in Somalia

1996

Italy cuts deficits to qualify for inclusion in the plans of the Economic Monetary Union

1998

Italy is declared eligible to adopt a common European currency, the Euro

Suggestions for Further Reading

Isaac Asimov, *The Dark Ages*. Boston: Houghton Mifflin, 1968. A history for young people that traces the various political movements during this period.

Michelle Berriedale-Johnson, *The British Museum Cookbook*. New York: Abbeyville Press, 1987. A discussion of the eating habits, providing a menu and some recipes of dishes of imperial Rome and Renaissance Italy.

Maurizio Forte and Alberto Silotti, eds., *Virtual Archaeology*. New York: Harry N. Abrams, 1966. A study of the trade carried on by the Etruscans is illustrated with maps showing possible trade routes. A selection of informative articles on ancient Italy covering Rome and Pompeii, as well as the civilizations of the Etruscans and other vanished peoples. Includes material on the Ice Man.

Genevieve Foster, *When and Where in Italy: A Passport to Yesterday for Readers and Travelers of Today*. New York: Rand McNally, 1955. Through words, maps, and pictures, the author re-creates twenty-six hundred years of history and shows the traveler what can be seen today from past eras.

——, *The World of Columbus and Sons*. New York: Charles Scribner's Sons, 1965. A biography of Christopher Columbus telling what life was like in his time.

Claudia Gaspari, *Food in Italy: International Food Library*. Vero Beach, FL: Rourke Publications, 1989. A book for young readers that contains recipes for Italian food and a description of customs.

Annaluisa Pedrotti, "Otzi: The Ice Man," in *Virtual Archaeology*, Maurizio Forte and Alberto Siliotti, eds. New York: Harry N. Abrams, 1996. Contributions from scientists involved in various kinds of studies has helped to reconstruct what the Ice Man and his equipment looked like when he was alive.

Jenny Ridgwell, *A Taste of Italy*. New York: Thomson Learning, 1993. A description of Italian food and customs for young readers.

Konrad Spindler, *The Man in the Ice*. New York: Harmony Books, 1994. The author led the team of international scientists who discovered the five-thousand-year-old body in the ice of the Italian Alps. This narration also tells what scientists are learning about the Stone Age from this remarkable find.

David Travis, *The Land and People of Italy*. New York: HarperCollins, 1992. A survey of the history and customs of Italy with good maps and photographs.

Michael Vickers, *The Roman World*. New York: Peter Bedrick, 1989. A book on the Roman and Etruscan civilization with many illustrations and maps.

James Wellard, *The Search for the Etruscans*. New York: Saturday Review Press, 1973. A well-illustrated book that focuses on the Etruscan civilization.

Örjan Wikander, "The Rise and Fall of Rome," in Göran Burenhult, ed., *Old World Civilizations: The Rise of Cities and States*. San Francisco: HarperCollins, 1994. This lavishly illustrated volume places Rome in the context of other civilizations.

WORKS CONSULTED

Jacques Bethemont and Jean Pelletier, *Italy: A Geographical Introduction*. London: Longman, 1983. The focus of this book is the geography and climate of Italy.

John Boardman, Jasper Griffin, and Oswyn Murray, eds., *The Oxford History of the Classical World*. Oxford: Oxford University Press, 1986. Eleven chapters by different scholars dealing with various aspects of Roman civilization.

Shepard B. Clough and Salvatore Saladino, *A History of Modern Italy: Documents, Readings, and Commentary*. New York: Columbia University Press, 1968. Translations and analysis of pertinent documents in the history of Italy from 1848 to 1966.

Vincent Cronin, *The Horizon Concise History of Italy*. New York: American Heritage, 1972. This well-illustrated book gives a short history of Italy from Rome to modern times.

Charles Dickens, *Pictures from Italy* (1845). New York: Coward, McCann & Geoghegan, 1973. The famous nineteenth-century English novelist gives his impressions of living in Italy.

Christopher Duggan, *A Concise History of Italy*. Cambridge: University of Cambridge Press, 1994. This brief history covers the period from 400 to modern times.

Eyewitness Travel Guides, *Italy* (1845). London: Dorling Kindersley, 1996. In addition to the many illustrations regarding specific places in Italy, the book has a good introduction to the history and accomplishments of the Italians.

Elaine Fantham, Helene Peet Foley, Natalie Boymel Kampen, Sarah B. Pomeroy, and H. A. Shapiro, *Women in the Classical World: Image and Text*. New York: Oxford University Press, 1994. This volume describes the role of women on the Italian peninsula, covering the Etruscan, Republican, and imperial periods.

Matt Frei, *Getting the Boot: Italy's Unfinished Revolution*. New York: Times Books, Random House, 1995. A survey of current conditions in Italy is reported by the BBC's southern Europe correspondent.

Michael Grant, "Time Stopped at Pompeii." In Joseph J. Thorndike Jr., ed., *Discovery of Lost Worlds.* New York: American Heritage, 1979. This article looks at Roman and Etruscan life. Good illustrations.

Richard Halliburton, *Richard Halliburton's Complete Book of Marvels.* Indianapolis: Bobbs-Merrill, 1941. In Chapters 22–26 this American adventurer describes crossing the Alps on an elephant as Hannibal did, visiting Rome and Pompeii, and swimming in the Blue Grotto.

Harry Header, *Italy: A Short History.* Cambridge: University of Cambridge Press, 1990. A brief history from prehistoric times to 1989.

Paul Hofmann, *That Fine Italian Hand.* New York: Henry Holt, 1990. The author, who was the chief of the *New York Times* Rome bureau, analyzes current life in Italy.

George Holmes, ed., *The Oxford History of Italy.* Oxford: Oxford University Press, 1997. This collection of articles traces the history of Italy from Augustus to modern times.

Tom Hundley, "Anti-Mafia Sweep Helps Sicilian Capital Clean Up Its Act," *Chicago Tribune*, April 22, 1998. This news account reports progress in Italy's attempt to deal with the Mafia.

Valerio Lintner, *A Traveller's History of Italy*, 4th ed. New York: Interlink Books, 1997. A brief history from the cave dwellers to current times.

Frances Mayes, *Under the Tuscan Sun: At Home in Italy.* New York: Broadway Books, 1996. An American woman buys a home in Tuscany and describes her life there.

Jan Morris, *The Venetian Empire: A Sea Voyage.* London: Penguin Books, 1980. A well-known travel writer traces the chief magistrates' domain from Venice itself to the territories the city controlled.

William Murray, *The Last Italian: Portrait of a People.* New York: Prentice Hall, 1991. The author, a former staff writer for the *New Yorker*, interviews a diverse selection of Italians.

Alice Leccese Powers, ed., *Italy in Mind.* New York: Vintage Books, Random House, 1997. This anthology explores the comments about Italy by writers of the past two centuries.

Colin Renfrew and Paul Bahn, *Archaeology: Theories, Methods, and Practice*. New York: Thames and Hudson, 1991. Archaeological techniques used in exploring Etruscan tombs and the effect of changing landscape environment are described.

Elizabeth Romer, *Italian Pizza and Hearth Breads*. New York: Clarkson N. Potter, 1987. This book of recipes tells the history of pizza.

Waverly Root, *The Food of Italy*. New York: Atheneum Press, 1971. The food of different parts of Italy is described and related to history.

Dennis Mack Smith, *Italy: A Modern History*, rev. ed., Ann Arbor: University of Michigan Press, 1969. An in-depth treatment of the history of Italy from 1861 to 1969.

Time-Life Books, eds., *Lost Civilizations Series*. Alexandria, VA: Time-Life Books. Good illustrations accompany text depicting life in these ancient civilizations. This material helps readers visualize life in these eras and understand the events that shaped the civilizations. *Etruscans: Italy's Lovers of Life* (1995); *Pompeii: The Vanished City* (1992); *Rome: Echoes of Imperial Glory* (1994).

———, *Time Frame Series*. Alexandria, VA: Time-Life Books. *Empires Ascendant* (400 B.C.–A.D. 200) (1989); *Empires Besieged* (A.D. 200–600) (1988); *The Human Dawn: Barbarian Tides* (1500–600 B.C.) (1987); *A Soaring Spirit* (600–400 B.C.) (1988).

———, *What Life Was Like When Rome Ruled the World: The Roman Empire: 100 B.C.–A.D. 200*. Alexandria, VA: Time-Life Books, 1997.

Bruce Watson, "This Is *Not* Your Father's Automobile," *Smithsonian*, December 1997. The author tries out a Ferrari and wishes he had one.

David Willey, *Italians*. London: British Broadcasting Corporation, 1984. The BBC correspondent in Rome produced this book based on the many interviews done for a ten-part TV series.

INDEX

107

PICTURE CREDITS

ABOUT THE AUTHOR

Leila Merrell Foster is a lawyer, minister, psychologist, and writer. She holds the degrees of B.S. in business administration, J.D., and Ph.D. from Northwestern University and M.Div. from Garrett Theological Seminary. In addition to professional books and articles, she has written nineteen children's books about countries, people, and issues.

Travel and photography are two of her hobbies. The first European country she visited was Italy, and she has returned to that country to see more of it. Another of her interests is archaeology, and Italy is a land rich in the story of early humans.